MW01244744

The Next

19 Days

Laurie Lindqvist
Karen Drevermann

For Mom and Dad.
You can stop worrying about us now.

Contents

Chapter 1
19 Days

What started out like so many other phone chats, suddenly became a life-altering conversation. "I found the sweet spot," Karen said in a way I've never heard her sound before. Something inside of me knew that she was about to tell me something profound, and probably not about a new bakery in town. Karen had my total attention as she began to tell her story.

Paul, Karen's husband, was in the midst of a paralyzing business crisis. It was tax time, yet again, and the weight of being a one man show in a physically and sometimes mentally challenging business was bearing down on him. She could hear the distress in his voice as he pleaded for her to please come help him. She wanted to help him, but didn't know how. As she stepped into the shower that morning, she was overwhelmed with a feeling of helplessness, and that's when in desperation she cried, "God, I don't know what to do."

She wasn't expecting to hear an answer. But God, The One and only Creator of Heaven and earth, *did* speak to her. Yeah, you heard me. God spoke to Karen! Sorry, no thunder, no lightning. He simply said, "An accountant will be at Paul's door at 2:00 p.m."

What did she just say? I thought to myself, as so many other questions raced through my mind: Was it an audible voice? Was she stunned? Had she taken any unusual medication that day? What happened next?

One moment she and I were chatting about how many delicious guilt clad carbs we had eaten that day, and in the next she blurts out, "God spoke to me!" But all I could say was "w...what?"

"I said w...what? myself," Karen answered. Is that you God? Did I hear that right? she wondered. Then, as she quickly got out of the shower with a sense of urgency, again she heard His voice. "Take your time, the accountant won't be there until 2:00 p.m." It was only 11:30 a.m., and she was pretty sure she had just heard the voice of God actually speak to her; what was she going to do with herself for the next two and a half hours? At 1:00 p.m., when she could stand it no longer, she jumped into the car and headed toward Paul's shop. She was excited and nauseous at the same time. "God, show me your glory. Show me your glory. Show me your glory," she repeated out-loud over and over as she drove as fast as she legally could.

I was hooked and on the edge of my seat as I continued to listen. I couldn't help but wonder if Paul was going to believe her or think she had lost her mind.

It turns out, he not only thought she had lost a few marbles somewhere along the way, but he was also kind of angry that she would come waste his time. Was he really supposed to stop everything and wait by the door hoping that it might be true? He wanted her to *physically* do something, make some calls or at *least* be stressed like he was, but she just continued to say, "God said an accountant will be here at 2:00 p.m." Somehow she convinced him to sit still and wait out the next thirty minutes; after that they could argue about who was or wasn't crazy. The 30 minute wait was painfully quiet. Karen could actually hear the tick tick tick of the battery operated clock on the wall as Paul seemed to grow more frustrated.

At exactly 2:00 p.m they heard someone walk in

the front door. This was the moment adult diapers were made for! Karen rushed out to see the accountant that she was so sure God said would be there. "It's just my landlord," Paul snickered and said, in a "hah! you *are* nuts" kind of voice.

It seems like this could have been the time she would have wanted to give up and think maybe she was wrong. But No! Determined she had really heard from God, and the fact that this landlord, who never before in 7 years came to the shop to pick up a rent check, had actually showed up at exactly 2:00 p.m. filled her with a stronger belief. "This guy has got to be connected to my promised accountant," Karen mumbled to herself.

While Paul and the landlord chitchatted about nothing in particular, Karen nervously spit out, "Do you know an accountant?" At first the landlord gave her a few names of some accountants he knew, and then finally her moment arrived. "I see you're working on your taxes," he said to Paul, and then added, "I was a bean counter for 30 years, can I help?" While Paul was still wondering what kind of beans he counted, Karen knew she was looking at her answer. It was just as God had said, an accountant *had* showed up at Paul's shop at 2:00 pm. She asked God. He answered. Angels singing! Suddenly, Karen was walking on air and would never be the same again. She couldn't stop herself from smiling for the rest of that day. Karen had had an encounter with God that would forever change her life.

This was all so amazing to me. How? After all, it's Karen, my somewhat normal sister. Karen, the sister who was convinced there was no way to get into her car when the battery in her car remote went out. She's no Abraham or Moses. How did she hear God's voice so clearly? Is it possible for me to hear God's voice, I questioned? How can I hear God? How could I have grown up in church and didn't know this was possible? I was filled with so many questions, but mostly I was overwhelmed with a deep wanting for whatever she knew or had that I didn't.

Thankfully, she believed she *did* know exactly how and why it happened. I was glued to the phone waiting to hear the answer as another story began.

"You know how we both long for a big amazing life?" she asked. And then she said, "If the Bible is all true, there must be more. We must be missing something." Her dreams were so big, but her life felt so small. She was done with knowing she was a "more than" girl living a "less than" life. Done with being a somebody feeling like a nobody. "Amen!!" I agreed. "Preach it sista!"

She began to wonder about who she knew that was living a big life. That's when our Uncle Dave came to mind. Uncle Dave was David Wilkerson, founder of Teen Challenge, a Christian drug rehab program birthed in New York City in the 1960s, and now worldwide. He authored *The Cross and the Switchblade*, the book that gave the account of his amazing story. He was our mom's oldest brother, and he was living a big life for God. What made him so different from me? she wondered. She knew that God directed his life, but she wanted to know the how part. This set her on a quest to find, not just the answer to how his calling came, but to figure out how to find hers.

She told me how she read the first chapter of Uncle Dave's book *The Cross and the Switchblade*, over and over and over again until she had an "aha" moment.

"Spill it!" I demanded. "It all—God sending Uncle Dave to New York and the rest, happened when he decided to turn off his TV and instead committed that time every night to spend alone, in prayer, with God," Karen answered. For Uncle Dave it was after only 19 days of prayer before God spoke to him in a life changing way. At first when she counted the days between when he committed his time to prayer, and the moment when he heard God speak, and discovered it was only 19 days, she was convinced it was a typo. A year and 19 days she could buy, but just 19 days—wow! So she decided to do exactly what he had done and commit time each day to be alone with

God. Though she wasn't in ministry or a prophet, she asked for and believed she could also have such a relationship. Almost immediately into her daily committed "God time," she too began to hear God's voice, and just 10 days later is when she desperately cried out to God in the shower.

Could it really be that easy? I wondered. I had been spending more time reading my Bible and in prayer lately, but not in a very committed same time each day kind of way, and not with the expectancy that I was now feeling.

I can't tell you what else we talked about on the phone that night because after that I couldn't hear anything else. My heart began to pound with excitement. I couldn't wait to hang up and go be alone with God.

I decided I would double up. I would spend morning time with God after taking my kids to school and then night time after putting them in bed. I read my Bible, prayed, listened to some great worship music and just kind of talked to God as if He was sitting right next to me during these hours.

Something amazing happened for me on the second day of meeting with God this way. It was not the voice Karen heard so clearly, but more like inspiring thoughts and ideas that didn't feel like my own. Creative ideas began to flow, and a promise of an amazing future was revealed. I excitedly called Karen to tell her what was happening, what I felt I was hearing from God. She began to cry as she heard me talk about the very same ideas God had given her. All along, she and I believed we were meant for something more, that something was missing, and now God was confirming it. It was Him we were missing.

This was the beginning, well not really the beginning—that's in the next chapter, but this was a major turning point. More like a giant leap forward. We had discovered a powerful key to reaching a relationship with God. It was the turning point that forever changed our lives.

Chapter 2

The Early Years

Since we're sisters, the beginning obviously started for us at birth. Well, at my birth. Karen is five years older, five inches taller and sometimes *she* thinks she's five times smarter.

We were preachers' kids and church became our whole life. It was the '70s and in our church everyone was known as sister this and brother that. It was the years of the Jesus movement, and for some reason many of them, the hip young seriously seeking after God, were drawn to our church and to our parents.

Mom, who they referred to as simply "Sis," became their teacher and they in turn became her groupies. They were called the Seekers and even had their own choir, also conducted by Mom, called the Luv Group. Like we said, it was the '70s.

Many of the Seekers often spent time hanging around our house. I was young and thought it was cool, but Karen was a teenager and felt she had to compete for Mom and Dad's attention, and that wasn't so cool. While the Seekers were "finding it," we were missing it and no one noticed. Dad was always dreaming big dreams and keeping busy. He knew how to build and run a church like a business. He was, and still is, very social, humorous, extremely generous, and always had a great measure of faith. Unfortunately, it's easy to get so wrapped up in works and lose sight of the importance of relationship. Mom had a great teaching gift, and even all these years later, the Seekers are still grateful for those days. But, back then when Mom wasn't surrounded by her groupies, who she continuously mentored, she was busy being a pastor's wife.

So, like many other children, we were always thinking of ways to gain our parent's attention and approval. I once took violin lessons in elementary school, not because I liked the violin, but because I knew my dad liked the violin. Apparently, my days of violin practice while lying on the couch watching television wasn't very convincing, so I gave it up. Karen tried to form her own small singing group comprised of her and her two best friends. Dad *did* actually let them sing in church one Sunday, but she didn't like it much when he introduced them as "The Agony Sisters." Now she says maybe it was a prophetic title, because the audience *was* in agony for the entire three minutes of their first and last performance.

For us, church was more of a social event than a spiritual one. Karen and I both recall a moment from those years when things could have changed for us. It happened while our youth group was on a retreat at our church camp. Karen and I were both there, but being five years apart in age we each hung around a different group. You know—same crowd separate click. Anyway, one evening as we all sat in a circle for our nightly rap-session, something powerful began to take place. While we can't remember the details of how it began, we do remember the collective weeping as everyone cried out for forgiveness and reached for more of God. In the midst of this spontaneous time of repentance, someone got up and put Dallas Holm's "Peace, Joy & Love" album on the stereo. All at once, the weeping turned into a massive eruption of sobbing teenagers falling on their knees as we all listened to Dallas Holm sing:

"Make me a new creature.
Let old things pass away.
I hear that you can do it.
But I don't know what to say.
Fix this broken vessel.
Mold this life of clay.
Put me back together.
Do it Lord today."

A door had been opened for something powerful to take place in our youth group, and we all left that retreat with a resolve to become the new creatures Dallas Holm sang about. But back home in our day-to-day lives, we were all so young and didn't know how to keep the momentum flowing. Unfortunately, our youth leaders didn't seem to have the foundation to help us. If only we could go back and tell our younger selves about the God we now know, a lot of pain and bad direction could have been avoided. We could fill a whole crazy book about our years of growing up, but then we would have to mentally re-live them, and that wouldn't be so much fun, so we'll just keep this chapter brief.

Things changed, you know—people fight, churches split, and children wander. What happened? Well, just like so many other shattered churches, you can imagine. I mean that literally. You're just going to have to use your own imagination here. One day our whole lives were completely wrapped up in our church, and the next it was all gone. When a fall comes and there's no strong foundation to hold you up—it's painful.

One of the good things that came out of our young church years was that our belief that God was out there somewhere never wavered. We had just enough "religion" in us to pray when we were sick or in trouble and to feel guilty for not going to church. The problem was that we didn't have our own personal connection to God. We were living on our parent's faith.

As the years went by, there were many opportunities for us to find God for ourselves. I remember buying every album that Keith Green, a contemporary Christian music artist, produced, and reading the inspiring book about his journey. I was so profoundly effected by his desperate search after God. I would play those music cassettes over and over again in my car with tears flowing as I sang along. Something was happening in me, but I didn't know what to do with it. Now I can see from afar that it was the Holy Spirit wooing me. About a year after that, a co-worker of my husband committed suicide. I had only just met him, but was devastated. I couldn't help but wonder, if I were closer to God would I have sensed this guys despair? I was filled with so many would've, could've, and should'ves.

My best friend at the time didn't know God at all, and when I tried to talk with her about what I was feeling, she couldn't relate. God was knocking on my door and I may have put my hand on the knob, but I didn't open it that day. Now I look back on those days and so many others and wonder why I didn't advance. What happened? Why didn't I desperately start chasing after God?

Karen had an even louder knock on her door. Only three months after having her second child, Karen discovered a lump in her breast. While those around her tried to convince her that it was probably nothing, Karen knew it was something more. When the doctor said cancer, she knew that she was spiritually unprepared for the situation. The lumpectomy, weeks of chemotherapy poured into the painful port surgically cut into her chest, followed by radiation was worse than she had imagined. And just when she thought it was over, a year and a half later, it was back. This time she went the more radical route. A mastectomy, reconstructive surgery and enough side issues to fill up a whole book. During this awful time in her life, Karen had just enough church girl knowledge to know God was with her, but not enough to free her from the fear.

When Karen could have been whining "why God why," instead she knew she was missing something. She had heard many stories of miraculous healing.

Those people seemed to know God in a way she didn't. Her cancer episode was another one of those many opportunities that should have pushed her straight down the road that we're finally on, but it didn't.

Chapter 3

Fix This Broken Vessel

We were sisters, yes, but our friendship and business partnership didn't begin until later—way, way later. Skipping ahead many years, I had been hired by a friend to do some interior design work in her employer's home. It was no small job, and I had just given birth to my first child and couldn't do it alone. I thought it was my idea when I called and begged Karen to help me out, but now I know it was clearly God's idea. The home we were hired to work on wasn't just any home, it was a very high end, art filled, museum type home—we're not talking velvet Elvis' either. It was the kind of home that you would expect to see interior designers lining up to get into. "How did we get here?" we sometimes wondered. We weren't exactly sure about the how or why, but it didn't really matter because we felt and acted as if we belonged there.

It was a dream job and we were good at it. As a team, together we laughed as much as we worked. For us, it became evident very quickly that we were not only meant to be business partners, but clearly famous interior designers as well. And then, as quickly as it began, it was over.

Now that we had a taste of success there was no stopping us. Only a few weeks later, in the middle of our second week in silversmithing 101 class, we decided this was it. We were destined to be prosperous jewelry designers. After only a few classes, it became evident that this might not be our best choice since we were more interested in the wearing than in the making of the jewelry. Just a day or two later, a new career would be chosen. It seemed home furnishings designers would be a great choice as our new occupation. No one could dare say that we weren't full of big dreams and ideas.

It wasn't until two unsaved strangers convinced us to wholesale our wares at an Atlanta Home Furnishings show, that we began to notice something wasn't right. We were so sure we were about to hit the jackpot and find the career, the big thing that we were meant for. So as we packed up the SUV for our long drive from Dallas; we had such high hopes and expectations that this would finally be it—the success we longed for. While Karen took her turn driving and we listened to our favorite CD, I silently began to pray. I asked God for a safe trip of course, and because I didn't want to limit our success, I asked God to let the outcome of our show be beyond what I could ever imagine.

When we arrived in Atlanta and turned onto a street named "Lucky Street," we were convinced it was a sign. Oy vey! It pains me to think about what silly girls we were back then. We were so full of hope and so proud of our designs as we set up our wares. Everyone who walked by would stop and say, "Wow, your stuff is great!" and we believed them.

After day one, we didn't get any orders, but we did rack up the compliments. We still had four days to go, so we didn't worry too much about it. We were having a lot of fun, so much fun in fact, that the girl manning the booth across from us said she wished her sister was there with her. Day two, day three, day four went by, and still no sales. It was our laughter that kept us going. Thank God for our sense of humor which we inherited from our dad. On the fifth and final day with not one order in hand, we were told that we were runners up for "Best of Show" out of the hundreds of booths. Another nice compliment, but without reward. We spent $2000 for this space, we deserved something. Karen says it was after that moment that she noticed me somberly walking off toward the vendor snack table. When she asked where I was going I said, "I'm going to eat $2000 worth of those free bagels."

We weren't laughing quite as much as the last orderless day wore down. And then, "Oh no!" flung out of my mouth. "God answered my prayer!" "What prayer?" Karen wondered aloud. I told her that I prayed that the outcome of the show would be beyond what I could imagine; only one or two orders I could imagine, but no orders was way beyond what I could ever imagine.

On the very long and quiet drive home it didn't take a rocket scientist to realize something was wrong. How could our stuff be so good and yet not one sale? It just didn't make sense. So we both agreed that we needed to take some time off and separately seek God for answers. After some questioning, begging, pleading and whining to God, we began to recognize the error of our ways. We would like to say it was an "aha!" moment, but it was more of a "duh" moment of revelation. Just as we had foolishly taken the advice from those two strangers to go to Atlanta, now we could see all too clearly that we alone had chosen our path. Without ever consulting God, we decided our career choice and expected God to get on board.

Thank God that He is a loving and merciful God. Even though it seems we were getting a much deserved punishing "timeout," we could have really messed up our lives. Now, years later and wiser, we can thank God for not allowing the success to come, because this was the moment that finally pushed us to seek after God.

God is good. He doesn't waste a thing. We may not have been meant to be famous interior designers, but He used it to bring us together as more than just sisters. And though Atlanta may have been a dud financially, we had such a great time together and it taught us many valuable lessons. Lesson one, don't do anything unless God says do it. Lesson two, be careful what you pray for. Lesson three, it's not possible to eat $2000 worth of bagels in one day.

When we got home, we surrendered our ideas and dreams over to God and finally began to seek after Him. We were now on a new mission, and began to each separately seek God in our own way. While Karen did her thing, I spent my time reading through an old children's Bible story book. I wanted to learn everything I missed during my childhood years and thought it would be the best place to start.

We've discovered that life seems to take us on a

circular road. You can either go around and around in the same circle, like the Israelites in the wilderness, or you can move in an upward motion like on a spiral staircase. We had been spending enough years going around and around. This was the moment we began moving upward. During this time I suffered a painful back injury. All the standard medications didn't work. So I went to a specialist, got an MRI and was told I would need surgery. Everything in me said No! to surgery. I would like to say it was because I was sure God said, "No surgery," but it may have been all the people that gave me their back surgery horror stories that persuaded me. It was the kind of pain I had never before experienced. No matter how I tried there was no way to ease the pain. Thank God I didn't know any drug dealers.

As I lay in bed one night silently suffering, flipping TV channels, (okay maybe not so silently), I happened upon Dodie Osteen, Joel Osteen's mom, giving her testimony of how the doctors had sent her home to die of cancer twenty something years earlier. She said it was God's Word that brought her healing. I was amazed as I listened to her tell of her unwavering faith and absolute confidence in the power of God's Word. She said she grabbed hold of her favorite healing scriptures and declared them out loud over herself daily. She didn't just stand on the Word verbally, she once actually put her Bible on the floor and literally stood on it as she shouted out her healing scripture. Not the usual protocol, but I'm pretty sure God had a good "you go girl," chuckle over that moment. Even though the symptoms lingered for quite awhile, she kept on believing, declaring and standing until her healing manifested.

Could saying a Bible verse have such power? If so, how come I was never taught that? But I was in pain now, and didn't have time to be ticked off about why I was a pastor's kid who spent a lot of church years in Sunday school and in youth group and yet didn't know about this power of the Word. I grabbed my Bible and found my verse and began speaking it out-loud. "Jeremiah 30:17 says, *For I will restore you to health and heal you of your wounds declares the Lord.*" My faith wasn't so big and I was still scared, but I believed what Dodie Osteen said was true.

I did some Biblical research and found a verse that said that God's Word was alive and active. I discovered it was more than just written words, it's God breathed. And it says that God's Word cannot go out and come back void. I could go on and on with the outcome of my research because I was having a serious "there's some powerful stuff in this book" revelation.

I didn't have surgery, and the pain continued, but I kept praying and saying my verse over and over. It took a few months, but healing did come. It's been years now and I'm still pain free. Anytime I feel the slightest twinge I stomp my foot and repeat that verse again.

Not too long after that, our Uncle Don Wilkerson, younger brother of David Wilkerson, and co-founder of Teen Challenge, came to Dallas. He was scheduled to be on a TBN broadcast hosted by Evangelist Steve Hill along with Freda Lindsey, co-founder of Christ for the Nations. Karen and I went with our mom to see him. During his interview segment, Uncle Don told another great story of the amazing power of God's Word.

It seems that a pastor in Johannesburg faithfully preached in a local park weekly. After speaking one day, a disheveled street person asked the pastor if he could have his Bible. The pastor explained that it was the New Testament, and asked the young man why he wanted it. "Well," he answered sheepishly, "the pages look very thin, and I want it to roll my own marijuana." At that moment the pastor had an inspiration from God. He said, "I'll give you the New Testament, if you promise to read each page before you smoke it." The young man agreed and went on his way. Two years later, the faithful pastor was in the park, when a clean cut young man approached him. "Do you remember me?" he asked. The pastor was perplexed, so the man told him his story. "I did what you asked me to do. Every time I smoked a page, I read it first. I smoked Matthew, I smoked Mark, I smoked Luke, and then John smoked me!"

We didn't know it then, but eventually we would not just be hearing more of those very cool stories, we would also soon get to experience them.

As we continued to separately seek God, Karen became very quiet and our communication became very limited. She needed to separate herself from all the outside voices. She wanted to be able to hear God leading and directing her path instead of the world. Parents, friends, the television, and yes, even loving sisters can try to steer you in one direction or another.

I mistook her quiet time as her distancing herself. I was hoping for our partnership, not just as sisters who had now developed a great friendship, but as business partners to go forward.

Then something shiny got dangled in front of me. My husband, Bjorn, and I were offered a chance to move to a beautiful vacation spot in the mountains of North Carolina. A friend had recently purchased a large land development. They had big plans to design, build and sell large vacation homes. My husband would be project manager and I would be their interior designer. They had tried to entice us a year earlier, but we declined. We had a newborn baby, and I was so convinced that Karen and I had a million dollar business on our hands. Now it was different, because I thought the sisters-in-business thing was over. I prayed and thought it felt right to go. Not because I clearly heard God say go, because I didn't know then that it was possible to hear God in such a clear way as I do now. Karen and I weren't talking much and my husband was hating his job. I was clearly hearing *his* voice say, "I want to go. Lets go." So off we went.

North Carolina was beautiful. We were living in a small tourist town, but Asheville was only thirty minutes away. We rented a brand new log cabin up high on a mountain. Not a log cabin like you might see in old western movies, well, maybe from the outside it looked that way, but inside it had all the modern conveniences you would want. The view—oh the view! We could see for miles. It was especially beautiful in the fall when all the leaves turned into vivid reds, oranges, and yellows, but not so great in the winter when we could feel the wind coming through the crevices in between the logs.

Everything seemed to be going pretty well for us, and then our short log cabin lease ran out and we needed to find a new place to live. Most of the homes in the area were income producing vacation rental properties and as fast as they hit the market, they were quickly scooped up. Only one house seemed to be available in our price range. It had a nice view and looked great from the outside. We were surprised it hadn't yet sold. But then we went inside. Oy! We couldn't decide what was worse: the cheap dark paneling, the creepy brown shag carpet, or maybe the vintage olive green sinks and tub. We were good at remodeling and usually could see the possibilities in a property, but this one was a mess. "Let's get out of here," we both agreed after a very brief tour.

We were running out of time and nothing seemed to be right. Then one day, while driving down the mountain, my singing along to a favorite worship CD abrubtly changed into a desperate prayer. "God, I know you love me. You know we need a place to live. Please make a way." Before I could say, "In Jesus name, Amen," my cell phone rang. It was my husband. "I just talked to the realtor, she's urging us to go back to the first house and look again. The seller is eager. She said we should make an offer." If I hadn't just been begging God for help, I may have declined. Instead I said, "Okay, let's go now!" I was a bit stunned, and yet quite happy about such an immediate answer to a prayer. This was a new experience for me.

On our second look, nothing was different except for the fact that this time I believed God seemed to be saying that this was the house. An inspector told us that everything was in good order so we moved forward. The seller took more money off the already reduced price. We moved in three weeks later.

Things were going well for me, which made it easy for me to settle into this new-found level of spirituality. Unfortunately, for so many, comfort can keep you from the superabundantly-far-beyond-all-you-can-hope-or-dream-for life that God has and wants for you. Comfort can make you think, "I'm good, I'm happy enough" instead of contending for more.

Fortunately, for both Karen and I, Karen was not comfortable at all. She was back in Dallas contending for more, still struggling and knowing that was not God's plan. For her, those never ending struggles meant something was still missing. There must be more. This is what led her to search out the path of someone who'd had a breakthrough and was living the big kind of life that she and I longed for.

Chapter 4

Mold This Life of Clay

We had only been in our new home for a few weeks when it happened—the phone conversation that changed my life. The night my sister told me about the key that changes everything. How Uncle Dave's life became a big God-filled amazing life after he discovered it, and how she heard God directly and very specifically speak to her because of it, and now I knew the key. How spending a daily committed time alone with God changes everything.

As I said earlier, it wasn't that I never spent time

alone with God, because I had; this was just different. It was the daily no-matter-what promise to be there. And it's more than just the doing. It's the doing, committing, with a spirit of expectation. Uncle Dave expected something, Karen expected something, and now I was nearly jumping up and down as I was completely filled with an excited spirit of joyful expectation.

When, on only the second day, I was getting inspired ideas I knew were coming directly from God, it made me all the more excited for what would come next. I wasn't hearing an audible voice, but I knew that I was hearing God. Words can't explain what it feels like when you know that God, the One and only, the Most High God, is speaking directly to you—it changes everything.

Each day I would drop off my kids and rush home to spend time in the "meeting place." Karen and I spoke to each other every single night after that. Our old mindless chitchats had become exciting conversations about what God was doing in and for each of us. How could we have lived all those previous years without knowing that we could not only talk to God, but actually hear from Him, encounter Him?

There's a Bible verse that says, *"Taste and see that the Lord is good."* Well, we now had a taste of God, and we wanted more. We couldn't get enough. Nothing else mattered. He had our total focus.

We used to think that to live our lives God's way meant that we would have to give up the things we wanted or enjoyed and live in a hut in some jungle as missionaries. Karen was even convinced that God would make her what she so desperately didn't want to be: a pastor's wife. And even worse, she thought God would make her marry the guy in our church who she disliked the most. Oh, how little we knew. It seems crazy now, but sadly we know that lots of church kids are raised to think this way. The truth is that God is nothing like we had foolishly imagined.

A couple of days after that life-altering phone call, Karen called and said, "I woke up this morning saying—Ephesians." "Okay," we agreed, "let's read Ephesians." Wow! What a powerful book. "Haven't we ever read this before?" we questioned. We actually had both read it probably many times before, but now it was different. Because we were spending time with God, it was as if our seeing and hearing, our understanding, had become sharper. We were reading it with new revelation. We soon realized that the more time we spent with God, the greater our perception. We would pick up and re-read a book we had read in the past, but now it was as if we had never read it before.

In Ephesians 1 there's a powerful prayer that Paul prayed that we began to pray over ourselves. It begins with, *"God grant me a spirit of wisdom and revelation in the knowledge of You."* As we continued to pray that prayer, God continued to answer.

If you were to look at my prayer journal from those days, you'll see that on every page I've written, teach me, guide me, show me, open my eyes to see and my ears to hear. I not only prayed it, but said it out-loud several times a day. It was as if blinders had been removed from our eyes and nothing could stop us now. We wanted to know about everything God wanted for us, about everything that we hadn't realized was possible.

Hosea 4:6 says, *"My people are destroyed from lack of knowledge."* As God began to reveal all of His promises, and teach us about the difference between what is blessing and what is part of the curse, we were stunned by how much we had suffered from our lack of knowledge. It felt like we were going back to school again. Not a physical school, but a spiritual school. It wasn't like going back to college, but more like kindergarten. We had to let go of all our preconceived ideas of who God is and allow Him to, as it says in Romans 12:2, *renew our minds.* And that was exactly what began to happen. We literally had to go back to "In the beginning... ."

The more He revealed Himself to us, the more questions we asked. The answers came in many ways: Sometimes through great books or a televised sermon, and at other times the answers would come in unusual or unexpected ways, but they were always confirmed through our Bibles. I specifically remember asking God if it was true that we should *always* expect healing. I told Karen that it has to be a yes or no. I said, "I can't pray if I have doubt." Suddenly, it seemed that every television minister was preaching on healing and quoting many Bible scriptures that confirmed what I had hoped. By the way, the answer was a definite YES!

But even though we were learning about *the more* that we had been missing, *the more* that the Bible says belongs to us, we didn't know how to go about getting it, how to make it all a reality in our day-to-day life.

Karen called one night to tell me that she had just heard a great sermon about God not wanting us to be living in any kind of lack. She knew that it was true, but when the speaker said, "God wants you to be blessed in every area of your life, you just need to *take it,"* Karen became annoyed because they didn't give directions on how to go about just taking it. "Just take it? What does that mean? How?" we each questioned. One day God would reveal something new and we would be overjoyed by the new revelation, and the next moment we would be crying, "When God? When are we going to see the manifestation of all these great promises?" We wanted it all.

We wanted it now! It's a good thing that we hadn't yet read 2 Peter 3:8 where it says that a thousand years is like one day to God.

I can't say that we were patient, because that would be far from the truth, but God would soon teach us everything we needed to know. We, of course, wanted the lessons to begin with the instant manifestation of all those great promises, but that's not how it happened. First, we had to go through some stuff, a transformation, a metamorphosis so to speak. We were like caterpillars that just realized they were supposed to be butterflies. You can't spend time in God's presence and not be changed, but there would be a process to reach that new identity. During those early months, the Holy Spirit began to change the way we thought, the way we talked, and the way we prayed. However, we would have to figure out who He, the Holy Spirit, actually was. We had much to learn. It wasn't easy, and I'm not exactly sure how it happened, but we were finally becoming those new creatures we sang about back in our youth.

Just a few months into our new journey, my husband found out that he was about to be out of a job. We discovered that our friends could no longer afford to keep building. It appeared we were in a crisis. We were about to be jobless. And now, we were living in a home that needed a complete renovation before we could even think about selling it.

"Okay God, what are you going to do about this?" I cried out. I expected Him to come through, but couldn't figure out the how part.

We knew it was time to go home. Home to Texas where we obviously belonged. No matter where we've gone in the past, it seems God always led us back to Dallas. I'm laughing as I write this thinking about how long it took me to get a clue. I thought I originally chose Dallas, but I'm seeing now that it was God who put me here. I was only nine years old when I knew I would one day live in Dallas. Uncle Dave invited and paid for the whole family, his brothers, sisters, and their families, to all meet in Dallas where he lived at the time, for a family reunion. *Our* family lived on Long Island in New York. I had never been further then Washington D.C. and was beyond excited. So excited that I went into praying overtime mode. The one thing I did learn in church during my youth was that "Jesus is coming back soon!" So I prayed day and night, "Jesus, please don't come back until I've been to Texas."

I did get my trip, and it left a big impression on me. Years later, after I graduated high school, Mom said, "Uncle Dave said that if you choose a college he would pay for your first semester." Thank God for a praying mom and a generous uncle. I, of course, chose a school in Dallas.

So here I was in North Carolina knowing it was

time to go back to Texas, and again, for the third time, Uncle Dave was somehow connected to my return to Dallas.

It was time to go. Only now, we had this unfinished house to deal with. I remember praying over and over, "Please God help us finish this place so that we can move on." We were overwhelmed by the amount of work that needed to be done. I'm sad to say my prayers may have been a little whiney during those days.

"Please God, make someone come to the door and offer to buy the place as is because I can't see how it can get done." The shag rug, the low ceilings, the creepy paneling, and so much more had me praying, "send a short blind person to buy this place." But God! He overlooked the sometimes whiney prayers and heard the real cry of my heart. The truth is that I had learned quite a bit over the past few months, and even though I whined a bit, I knew that God always wants the best for me. If I would just trust Him and keep claiming what the Bible says, He would absolutely come through. The next thing I knew, I was telling Karen that I didn't know how, but somehow the projects were getting completed. The painting, putting in new floors, new ceiling, new bathrooms and so much more. Thank you, God!

Finally, the house was complete and ready to put on the market. We didn't have time to sit around and wait for a buyer. We had to start packing and get going. What about a job, and where would we live? We had no idea. We literally packed up to move on prayer and faith alone.

About a week before we moved, Bjorn looked on the internet and quickly picked out a house to rent. The coolest part was that I had promised my two young boys, Leif and Zack, that we would find a home with a playground. Although it seemed like a pretty big promise for someone who knew there was no job, no house, and only about a months worth of money to live on, God came through. I love the way He does that. Our last minute, random rental home choice happened to be on a greenbelt. The backyard gate opened up onto a park complete with a playground. Yay, God!

The day we packed the moving truck, my husband received a totally unexpected call. It was his previous boss from Texas. He said, "Bjorn, I heard you were moving back to Texas. Do you need a job?" And just like that, God completely came through in a last minute kind of way, which He seems to enjoy doing. We just needed to keep moving forward and trusting God.

I've heard that satan isn't much bothered with us when we're busy making a mess of our lives, living in the dark, but as soon as we begin to see and move into light, all hell breaks loose. We must have been doing something right at that moment, because just as we were about to pull away from where we no longer belonged, and set out for our place of destiny, an unexpected battle hit.

First, when Bjorn put some mouse poison around the outside perimeter of the house as we were leaving, both our cat and dog immediately found it and began to eat it. After some vomit inducing panic filled moments, we prayed over our pets and put them in the truck because we had to go. Then, as we drove down the road and out onto the highway hoping and praying that our beloved pets would live and not throw up in the truck, our next unexpected moment happened.

I was driving Bjorn's truck while he drove a rented moving truck that took us days to pack. It was late on a Friday night, and just as we got onto the highway and were beginning to settle in for our long drive to the halfway point where we would stop for the night, the moving truck broke down. We weren't just anywhere on the highway either, we were stopped on the tight and windy gorge portion of the highway. "Really? Is this happening now?" I loudly spoke into the wind. I totally believed it was a spiritual attack, but all I could think of was how long it took to squeeze everything into that truck. And how it was late on the weekend, and all the local U-Haul businesses were closed. As large 18-wheel trucks dangerously sped by nearly blowing us off the road, we nervously laughed, what else could happen? Instead of waiting to find out, I began to pray. I called Karen and asked her to pray as well. The more I looked at the situation, the more righteous anger began to build in me. My prayers got louder and more fervent. The highway noise was so loud, and my husband was in the truck on the phone with U-Haul, so no one besides Heaven and hell could hear me. I had learned a few things about prayer over the past few months, about putting a demand on the Word, so I took authority and commanded help from Heaven as I demanded hell to back off.

Our boys watched movies on their DVD players and seemed not to be phased by any of it. After four hours, help arrived from a town nearly two hours away. It was a simple ten minute fix and we were on the move. Thank you, God. We were exhausted, but determined to at least make our way to the next state.

Our helpers had to drive in our direction for about an hour and a half before their turnoff. Instead of rushing off, they wanted to make sure we were okay, and like angels guiding us, they escorted us all the way out of North Carolina. God is good.

Chapter 5

The Keys

Finally, back to Texas where I clearly belonged. Karen and I still continued to communicate by phone. We may have both been geographically living in Dallas, but we lived in separate suburbs about a forty-five minute drive apart. We laugh because we are convinced that one day we'll sit across the big board room table of our future company where we'll be in the midst of an important business meeting, and even though we're sitting in the same room, we'll have to turn our chairs around and phone one another because that's how we best communicate.

Now that I was back in Texas, Karen and I were

convinced that this was our moment—the moment God was going to deliver on the promise, the blessing, the calling, the dream. Now we're ready. Here it all comes, we naively thought. We didn't just want it, we needed to see those tangible things that come from being God's kid. We didn't quite get it yet, the way God works, the pattern, the order, the plan God has to get us from who we were to who He wants us to be.

Looking back now, Oy! We roll our eyes over the thought of our former selves. Much of our painful impatience, suffering and whining came from our sad state of ignorance. Whoever said ignorance is bliss is totally ignorant.

God had already taught us so much. So after a while, we were convinced that we must now know it all; the training was over and the big life would begin. We wanted the big plans God had for us to get started, and just in case we didn't yet know it all, we asked for "on-the-job" training.

What we had was just the beginning, a "Getting to Know God 101" course. God was just beginning to build our foundation, but our problem was that we kept wanting to decorate the rooms.

We were always wanting and expecting something big to happen. We just didn't know what it would be. We would start all our phone conversations with "anything?" "Not yet. Anything on your end?" And even though it often felt like nothing was happening, God was always doing something. God continued to build our foundation even while we impatiently kept looking for the "big thing." We didn't realize that in the small things, big things *were* happening.

Usually it would begin with something subtle or weird like when Karen said, "I don't know if it means anything, but I keep getting or seeing the number 222." The clock always read 2:22 when she looked at it or she would get change of $2.22 or go to an address of 222. Call us crazy if you want, but God often uses different ways to speak to us, and it wasn't the first time that a number or name or something else unusual would keep coming up until we got the message.

So, after some time of 222 happening, Karen said, "I think I might know what it means." Then she told me a nutty story about her daughter's pet hedgehog. Spike, the hedgehog, was an important member of their family and he was getting weak and maybe dying. Hedgehogs don't have a long life expectancy, and they had already had him for over two years. So Karen decided the 222 must obviously mean that Spike was going to die at two years, two months, and two days old, which was only days away. "Okay, maybe," I said in a less than convinced way. I was new at this thing of being sensitive to the many ways

God speaks, and I wasn't about to second guess what God might be saying. Of course, that wasn't it at all. I can't remember the exact number of months and days until Spikes death but it wasn't two years, two months and two days. The 222 continued even after Spike's sad death, and normally, once we get the meaning, the continuing clue stops.

When we were together on Easter, Karen handed me a book titled, *Authority in Prayer,* by Dutch Sheets, an internationally known author, teacher, and revivalist. She said, "I felt like I was supposed to buy us both this book." Later that night, while we both were home reading our books, Karen called me and excitedly said, "Did you read it yet?" "I started to," I answered. "But did you read page 71 yet!?" she wanted to know. I told her that she was reading faster than me and I was still a few pages behind her. So we agreed that I would call her back as soon as I caught up. Evidently, there was something important on that page that she wanted me to read, but the book was really good and I didn't want to skip over anything, so I kept on reading. Then my heart started beating fast as I read on page 71 about how God was putting the number 222 over and over in front of Dutch Sheets. He wrote that he knew it was God speaking to him about Isaiah 22:22. Isaiah 22:22 says, *"I will place on his shoulder the key to the house of David; what he opens no one can shut, and what he shuts no one can open."* This was definitely way cooler than a hedge-hog's time of death. At the time, Karen and I had both been reading different books on authority and knew it was a word for us. It was exciting to know God was speaking to us about something new. And almost as great as getting that word from God, was the fact that we could now say, "See, we're not crazy. God sometimes talks to Dutch Sheets in the very same weird way he often speaks to us." About a week later, Karen asked if I had been getting any literal keys. At first I said no, because nothing came to mind, but then—"Yes! I did get a key this week!" I remembered. I told her about the day I was in the playground with my boys when one of their little friends, Sheldon, came over and handed me a key. He said, "I found it." I said, "Okay, thank you," and never thought anything else about it. Karen sug-gested I ask God about what the key meant. For a day or so I kept asking, "God, what's the key? What's the key?" Then one night as I was reading a book, suddenly the words **Worship is the key** seemed to leap off the page at me. My heart started to beat fast, as it always does when I get a word from God, and I knew it was my answer. Worship is the key!

So, I began to read every book about worship that I could get my hands on. I learned that worship is the key to entering into God's presence. That worship is also a form of warfare. Worship was the great

51

weapon that David wielded in the Bible. Worship is an act of love, and completely changes the atmosphere. We knew that worship was very important, we just didn't yet realize how important. We had the head knowledge, but we still needed a revelation.

About a week after receiving the first key, my family and I were driving to an art festival in Fort Worth when a new key arrived. My three year old son reached into his car seat and grabbed a hold of something. "Here's a goldfish," he said while proudly handing it to me, and then reached for more, but this time he said, "Here's a key." He handed me a little silver key. My heart started to beat fast. "I've got to call Karen!" I exclaimed, reaching for my cell phone. "I just got another key!" I practically screamed into the phone. I told her I would call her back as soon as I knew what the key meant. As we strolled through the many artists booths up and down Main Street, Fort Worth, I kept my eyes and ears wide open expecting to receive some kind of revelation as to what this key meant. No secret messages written in the oil paintings and no clues hidden in the pottery, but when my three year old grabbed a couple of metal balls off of a moving sculpture I did get *that* message. The "it's time to leave now" message.

On the way home I didn't have much time to think about the key because there were two little restless boys in the back seat about to turn into monsters. If they didn't get food and fun in the next few minutes the outcome could get ugly. Just before we turned off the road to get to the closest McDonalds, I looked to my right, and found myself staring at a giant word "KEY" written on the side of the trailer stopped next to us at the light. Then I noticed that over on the opposite side of the highway were two 18-wheelers parked in a field, and they also had the word "KEY" written very large across each trailer. The really interesting part was when I realized that this was the very same stretch of road that we were on earlier that morning when my son handed me the key. We were in the very same place, but on the opposite side of the highway.

In the early days of God speaking this way to us, Karen and I sometimes had a difficult time catching the meaning of the message, which was mostly because of our lack of knowledge. Sometimes we really enjoyed solving the mystery, and other times it would make us restlessly impatient. We've since had a "duh" breakthrough realizing that we don't have to have many nightly phone meetings pondering all the possible scenarios—as in the Spike will die in two years, two months, and two days. All we have to do is ask God and wait on the answer because He always leads us to it. We also now have more knowledge, wisdom, and understanding in the way God moves, which helps us get to the answer God wants us to see.

Just a few nights later, during one of our lengthy phone conferences, the answer came. Another great reward to our perpetual phone powwows is that the more we talk, the more we remember. We remember many things that we might have looked past, things that one of us thought were unimportant, but the other can see the connection. As we were talking, a silly memory came to mind.

I was alone in the car driving down that same stretch of road many months earlier, when I noticed that on each side of the highway, directly across from each other, were two very similar white church steeples. For some weird reason, it brought back to my mind a Dallas radio station contest from many years ago. A key was hidden somewhere in Dallas, and the radio station would give out weekly clues to where it might be. The person who found the key would win a BMW. So all these years later, as I was driving past those two steeples, I said to myself, "if the clue was the key is between the two steeples, I would know where it was—on Highway 121." Then of course, I also thought to myself, what's wrong with me? Why am I thinking about some silly useless thought like that?

But God, He doesn't waste a thing. Karen and I realized that we had the answer. Could God have given me a weird thought like that so many months earlier because He actually planned to place a different kind of key for me to find there? Oh yes He could, and *did* in fact.

"Highway 121! One-to-One!," Karen blurts out. Because suddenly we saw it, the highway that my son handed me the key on was just down the road on the very same Highway 121 that's between the steeples. Highway 121 at Hebron Road, to be exact. And what does "Hebron" mean? It means friendship with God. God was telling us about the importance of being one-to-One with Him. The meeting place, our friendship with Him, our one-to-One time was the key.

Worship and one-to-One. Our worship time, and our one-to-One time alone with God, are the keys. The keys to not just all we need and desire, but to what God desires as well.

Yes, it seems all so obvious now. Obvious that time alone with God and in worship of God is the key, and that worship and that one-to-One are the very keys that King David held. But for two girls in a desperate seeking after all God has and wants for them, it was a valuable lesson of what's most important to God. You can be filled with knowledge of God, memorize the entire Bible, know all the biblical principles, and yet, not know God at all. It's in that place of one-to-One time alone with Him, in God's very presence, where He imparts wisdom, knowledge and understanding to us. It's the place of revelation. It's where we receive his council and are charged with his power. It's not just the knowing about God that we need, it's truly knowing Him. It's not just a one time or sometimes deal. It's a relationship that has to be continuous and always growing.

Karen and I have the keys. The keys to open doors that no man can shut and to shut doors that no man can open. That's a power that only comes through the meeting place, our time of worship, and prayer alone with God.

Even though Karen and I often have a good laugh over the original idea of what she first thought the 222 meant, something truly amazing actually came out of the story of Spike's death.

Weeks before Spike began to get weak, Karen had a vision, a snapshot run through her mind, of her daughter playing on her bed with a little white kitten. Karen has had this interesting gift since she was very young. She would get a snapshot, a sudden picture in her mind and then it was gone. To her it was just a thing that happened. She thought it was normal and that everyone must have it. It wasn't until she began to desperately seek God, that she realized it was more. It was a gift. She told me that she even had a vision of herself bald long before she found out she had cancer. So now after Spike died, Karen knew that her daughter was in need of a new pet to care for. She also knew that she, Karen, was highly allergic to cats. But the vision!?

The white kitten vision had to be real. She decided to pray that God would find her daughter a specific cat that she, Karen, wouldn't be allergic to. *Instead*, God said, "Why aren't you praying that your allergies are healed!?" Yikes, how could she be so stupid? When she told me she was praying for that special non-allergy-inducing cat, I missed it too. We were both stunned by the fact that neither of us considered praying for the *best* solution. It was a shocking eye opener. Another "duh!" moment. What else were we missing? What else were we settling for?

"Okay God, I believe for my healing," Karen said, "But when will I know it's done so that I can go get a kitten for my daughter?" She heard God say, "If you believe you're healed, go get your kitten." It happened to be pet adoption week at the local shopping center, so off they went to find their new furry family member. Karens daughter, Katie, said the one thing she knew for sure was that she didn't want a white cat. That was interesting since the cat in Karen's vision was white. Karen decided to not say anything, but to just wait, watch, and see what happened. As they looked over the many cute cats and kittens, a particular kitten caught Katie's eye. It wasn't just any kitten either, it just so happened to be the only white kitten. Out of all those cute little critters, she was immediately drawn to this one. She remembered what she had said about not wanting a white cat, but there was just something about this little guy that had her sold. Even his name was special—Spirit.

Before they had a chance to pull out of the parking lot with Spirit, Karen was sneezing. Instead of questioning God, because she knew without a doubt that He promised her she was healed, she began to fight those lying symptoms away. The truth is that Karen didn't need to hear God confirm her healing, because she knew His Word says, "By Jesus stripes we *were* healed." Not "are going to be," but WERE! Our healing was completed the moment Jesus went to the cross for us. We just need to know the truth and claim it. But in this case, for Karen, God's confirmation gave her just enough extra righteous anger over her symptoms to fight no matter what. It was a pretty big battle. The symptoms seemed to be the worst she had ever faced. But determined, Karen would sometimes rub Spirit's little furry body right into her face as she loudly declared, "BY JESUS STRIPES, I AM HEALED!" Over and over every day she declared that verse until the symptoms disappeared. Hallelujah! After three and a half weeks of some sleepless suffering, it was done. She had won the battle.

This was a great lesson for both Karen and me.

While I may have been spared the actual painful suffering part (thank you, Jesus) we both learned many important things. Always expect God's best for us. Know and believe that all God's promises are true. Don't be thrown if symptoms linger. Fight! And most important, God is *always* good.

Chapter 6

God Said...WAR!

It was a good thing that we had some battle training behind us because God was about to give us a lesson in using it. While out shopping in another town, I ran into an old friend named Kelly. Neither of us lived in that town and it was weird to run into each other in that particular place. It wasn't my first "Kelly" encounter either. I had also been getting mail in my mailbox for someone named Kelly. At the same time that I was having my Kelly happenings, Karen was seeing red. No, she wasn't angry, she was actually seeing the color red. When she dropped her son, Andrew, off at school, she asked, "Why is everybody wearing red today?" He wasn't seeing what she was seeing, and simply said, "I don't know what you're talking about." For her, it was so pronounced—it was loud. Then on her way home it seemed like every car on the road was also red. When Karen and I discussed our consecutive occurrences, we laughed because we both thought, "if it's weird, usually it's God." We quickly looked up the meaning of the name Kelly. It meant war. Kelly and red both equaled war. Okay, we knew some stuff about warfare, we had each been reading up on it, but "what about it, God?" we questioned.

A few nights later, as I was reading through a new book, something I read seemed to ignite the answer. "WAR!" I said out-loud to myself. My heart started beating fast. It was late, and I didn't want to call and wake Karen, but my heart wouldn't stop beating so fast. When Karen gets a word from God she begins to cry. When I get a word, my heart beats fast and I want to jump up and down. It's an involuntary action for both of us. When it happens we know we are truly hearing God and not just thinking our own thoughts. It's another one of those things that continually amuses us. Just as we imagine ourselves in that future board room together, communicating only by phone, we also imagine her crying and me jumping up and down while our future employees say, "there they go again, they must have heard from God."

Finally, after not being able to settle down, I knew I had to call Karen. "WAR!" I shouted into the phone, "God says, WAR! the verb, the action, He's telling us to war." Immediately Karen began to cry as we received a revelation of what God was telling us to do.

We wanted everything to just drop into our laps, but God told us to WAR! He had trained us to fight, and now it was time to do some fighting. We were fighting for all that belongs to us: for our inheritance, for our health, for our prosperity, for our identity, for our destiny to come forth. We became two serious spiritual fighting sisters complete with swords and all. Yea, that's right, we had us some swords. They may have been plastic, but they were just that extra thing we needed to put us into true battle mode.

For us, warring means knowing what we are specifically fighting for, finding every Bible verse that confirms it, and declaring those words (God's Word) in prayer and out-loud until the answer comes. Warring also means that any time doubt may try to creep in, we shut it down by praising God and thanking Him that the answer is coming even if we can't yet see it.

Crazy Karen once took her sword with her as she walked to school to pick up her daughter. She was in one of those rare "nobody get in my way because I'm a mighty warrior on a heavenly mission" modes. Thank God nobody noticed her wielding her weapon through the air as she spoke out words of war, before God suddenly gave her a picture of herself. What should have been a covert mission turned out to be a little too overt. While I'm sure God enjoyed watching her zeal, mercifully He stopped her from facing what could have been a seriously embarrassing situation. She quickly shoved her plastic sword down the side of her sweatpants and walked the rest of the way to school with just a slight limp.

We knew we weren't fighting flesh and blood. Like it says in the book of Ephesians, the battle is always spiritual. It's not people we fight, but the spirit operating through them. Even though we sometimes waved a physical sword, we knew our real weapon was the living Word written in our Bibles.

We spent a good few weeks in warrior mode calling in our promised inheritance. We declared, decreed, and confessed every biblical promise we had knowledge of.

An interesting thing happened to me in the middle of calling forth my inheritance. My mom called and said that the next time I visit them, I could bring home George. George is an oil painting—a very old painting of an unknown guy we named George that has been in the family since I was very young. It's the one and only thing I requested to be mine in my parent's will. They were planning to sell their house and move from Texas to South Carolina where our younger sister lives. They didn't have a buyer yet, and they didn't offer my other siblings anything they requested, but for some unusual reason, I had been offered an early piece of my inheritance. Do I think it was because I had been warring for my inheritance? It wasn't the inheritance I had in mind, but yes! I think it was a physical manifestation that happened because of the warring. I'm not sure if it happened by way of a biblical principle or because God was just showing me that my warring and praying was working. Either way, it was encouraging.

It's often said that hindsight is 20/20. At the time, we didn't see what we can so clearly see now. Our time of warring had broken us through into a new place. It started with God telling us that it was time to get a Kingdom revelation. Everything God had taught us, everything our future would hold, was about the Kingdom of God. We needed a Kingdom revelation. So, as we did whenever God was teaching us about something new, we read every great Kingdom book that we could get our hands on. We even re-read Dutch Sheets' book *Authority in Prayer*, but this time it was as if we were reading it for the first time. Karen said, "He should rename the book *Kingdom Authority*, because that's what it's *really* about." When God moves you into a place of greater perspective you see everything as if you had two completely new eyes. Everything becomes clear. We were able to read our Bibles with greater understanding.

Then one night Karen called while I was making dinner. Usually we wait and talk at night when the kids are in bed, so I knew something was up. "I think it's time to make some t-shirts and necklaces," she suggested, and wanted to know if I was feeling the same thing. Why t-shirts and necklaces? Well, it's a very small part of a much larger future dream. A dream that includes, among so many other things, a calling to reach teenagers and college age kids. Karen and I have always had a desire to grab hold of kids that age and point them in the right direction. To give them what we missed, even *before* we actually knew all that we had missed.

We've known for many months exactly what those t-shirts and dog-tag type necklaces would say, but we didn't know when and where we would need them. I told Karen that I wasn't sure if it was time, but I would ask God to confirm it with me before I was willing to take a step forward. I asked my husband to watch the food on the stove while I went out for a brief walk. Outside, I said, "God if it's You, and it's time to design and produce these t-shirts and necklaces, please confirm it with me." I was afraid that I might miss the answer or confuse it with my own thinking if it wasn't very obvious, so I said, "God, if we're supposed to do this thing you're going to have to place a t-shirt and a necklace or an actual dog tag in an unexpected place in front of me." It was a bold request, but only moments after asking, as I turned the corner into the park, I SAW IT—a t-shirt! It was just lying there under a tree. "God, am I crazy or is that for me?" My heart started to beat with excitement as I ran home to call Karen. By the way, that very tree that I found the t-shirt under, God later used several times to speak to me in different ways. God is just cool that way.

I told Karen about what had just happened and that the t-shirt was a go, but I didn't get anything yet about the dog-tag necklace pendants. Then I reached into my purse to grab a pen, but instead, grabbed a hold of something I couldn't identify. I started to laugh out-loud when I pulled from my purse a shiny gold dog tag. Weeks earlier we had taken our dog to the vet for some vaccinations, and I had forgotten that I had thrown her rabies tag into my purse. Coincidence? Of course not. God knew it was there for me to find just when I needed it.

Only a few weeks later, Karen and I sat at my dining room table staring at a box full of t-shirts and a pile of necklaces. Each one had the bold declaration "I AM WHOSOEVER" written across them. This was one of the first revelations God had given Karen so many months ago when she first began to hear His voice. She had been reading Mark 11:23, *"For verily I say unto you, That **Whosoever** shall say unto this moun-*

tain, Be thou removed, and be thou cast into the sea; and shall not doubt in his heart, but shall believe that those things which he saith shall come to pass; he shall have whatsoever he saith." She was confused by how this verse could be possible. As she again began to mull over that verse, she heard God clearly say, "You are Whosoever." Karen began to cry as the revelation took hold and she declared out-loud, **"I am Whosoever!"** now believing it was indeed possible. We are the Whosoevers written about in the Bible. We are the Whosoevers, as in John 3:16, that believe Jesus is the Son of God who came to save us and set us free. We are the Whosoevers, as in John 4:14, who drink of the living water, who spend one-to-One time getting knowledge and revelation in His presence. We are the Whosoevers, as in Mark 11:23, who speak to and move mountains.

As we sat admiring our first product not quite sure about what was to come next, we asked, "What now God?" Are we going to sell these or give them away? How? Where? To who? When? As usual, we were hoping for something big and amazing.

In June, just a few weeks after we sat at the dining room table wondering "what next?" we were on our way to a meeting in Waco. While browsing through a book store, my eye went straight to a book with a title that spoke to me. I recognized the author. I bought it. It wasn't until I began reading it that I discovered it wasn't the author I thought it was, but someone with a similar name. Picking up that book was no mistake. It wasn't the first time God led us to a book this way. Our "I don't know what made me pick up this book" talks, turned into, "I guess God wants me to read this one."

Cindy Jacobs was the author; *The Supernatural Life* was the title. I didn't know who she was when I picked up the book, but I wanted to know her when I finally put it down. We found out that she would be speaking at a meeting in Waco, Texas. Waco was not far away, so we made plans to go. In all these many months of seeking and schooling we hadn't been on any field trips, so this was exciting.

Just in case this had something to do with the answer we were looking for, we brought the t-shirts and we both wore our necklaces. Karen even wore her Holiness Shirt. The "Holiness Shirt?" Well, that's a funny story we won't soon forget. Karen was shopping for some new shirts in a store with her husband one day, and when she came out of the fitting room after trying on several shirts, he said, "So are you only wearing white now?" "What?" she answered a bit confused. That's when she realized that all the shirts in her hand just so happened to be white. He, for some insane reason, assumed that all of her seeking after God had caused her to now wear an only white wardrobe—a special "Holiness" wardrobe. Did he really think that the girl who loves to wear body slimming black so often could actually go there?! Karen said she laughed hysterically all the way home. Seriously, is it just us? Why does our diligently seeking God make others think we're crazy? We would laugh about imagining the family planning an intervention. Even though it sometimes seemed funny, it was also quite sad. What now felt normal and vital to us, was looked at as fanatical to others. Thank God we always had each other to keep pushing us forward. Still, we often prayed, "God, vindicate us."

As we pulled up in front of the church, which is right on the main highway running through Waco, Karen began to laugh. The church that this meeting was being held in was the very same church that Karen once drove by, and seeing a banner announcing "Drive-Thru Service," she pointed and said, "I'm never going to *that* church." I started to laugh as I reminded her of when she once needed money and prayed that God would let it come from anywhere but a certain family member, and that was the very person it came from. And when she decided that she would never send money to a particular ministry, God prompted her to send them a hundred dollars. I told her that she better stop saying never because God doesn't seem to be agreeing with her "nevers."

The meeting wasn't exactly what we had expected. We had actually crashed a semi-private gathering. Cindy Jacobs happened to be the speaker at this meeting of the Texas branch of the Reformation Prayer Network. Karen and I have the gift of looking like we belong, so nobody seemed to notice or care that we weren't actual members. The worship music was great and we enjoyed hearing the details of what this group of prayer warriors was all about. We have heard many doom-and-gloom prophetic words from other prophets, but this time it was different. When these people got a prophetic word of some type of harm that could affect our nation, instead of just expecting it to happen, they get together and send out a call to prayer.

As we listened to the accounts of the many warnings they had received and that after warring in prayer these situations were averted or overturned, we were pretty excited. This was the kind of stuff we wanted to hear and see. Just as we had learned that we no longer had to take the garbage, anything considered as part of the curse of this world in our own personal lives, now we were introduced to an amazing God-loving group of people who were charged with the responsibility of warring by using fiery arrows of prayer pointed toward very specific targets. They were fighting for the safety and blessing of our nation. It was pretty cool.

When Cindy began to prophesy, it got really exciting. This is our moment, we thought! We expected to hear Cindy call out our names or even just refer to us as "The sisters with a big call on their lives." The audience was small, and she seemed to have a prophetic word for almost everyone but us, so we were a bit discouraged. "God, all this amazing stuff you are doing in us, doesn't anyone else see it?" When we had a chance to get in line for prayer, we maneuvered ourselves as close to Cindy as possible. God speaks through her in mighty ways, surely she's going to have a prophetic word for us, we thought. "Stay out of his line," we whispered to each other when we noticed that everyone that Cindy's husband prayed for was hitting the floor. We've seen it before, we just weren't looking to get it. We made it to the front of the line, and as we hoped, Cindy did pray for us, but nothing. No angels-singing-miracle-working prophetic words for us.

Thank God we're always praying for wisdom and revelation, because we are always in need of it. On the way home, as we talked it through, we began to feel kind of stupid as we quickly began to see the error of our ways. Good thing that nobody there happened to know us. Here we were, asking and learning to hear God's voice; what made us think we needed to get a word from someone else when we were able to get it straight from God? There's nothing wrong with receiving a prophetic word from someone. There are many who hear from God themselves that also often receive prophetic words from others, but we knew that in our specific case, because we were still in the midst of "the process," God was making sure that we didn't follow or look to anyone else. The Holy Spirit was the only mentor and voice God would allow us to hear.

Did God send us to that meeting? Maybe not. In our hope to receive a word of confirmation from someone else, and just the joy of getting out of the house, we're pretty sure it may have been all our own doing. But because God is always good, He allowed us to enjoy ourselves and learn our lessons in an anonymous way instead of in an embarrassingly public way.

Every time we've tried to get ahead of ourselves, God mercifully pushes us back in line. We believe it's because we have a *special order*. A few years ago we heard a pastor preach a sermon with a fast food restaurant analogy. He said that when you're in the drive-thru and you have a regular order, you quickly move through the line, but when you have a *special order*—this was the point where the audience began to hoop and holler as the organist added a little flair, and then again he repeated, "When you have a *special order* you have to pull over, park, and wait in the *special order* spot." Clearly, we have a seriously special

"special order," we concluded, because we felt like we had been in that special order spot for a *very* long time. Sometimes we laughed because we thought we must be in the "special order line" of a restaurant that hadn't even been built yet.

It may not have been our assignment to go to that meeting in Waco, but just a few weeks later we *were* assigned to attend a different meeting. This time we knew it was God. When we say "different," we're not *just* referring to the fact that it wasn't the same meeting.

On a Sunday morning, we were on our way to Denton, Texas to attend Chuck Pierce's church. Let's just say that it was like no other service we had ever attended. Chuck Pierce is a prophet, and he and Dutch Sheets have partnered in many amazing God-directed adventures together. We had read many of his books, but to see him in action, well, that was a whole other kind of thing.

This was our first close-up and personal adventure in a flag waving, shofar-blowing, multiple-prophet-speaking church service. It was a good thing we had released our old religious ways of thinking or we may not have survived. We weren't so much shocked by it as we were maybe a little stunned, especially during the "Shift" song when after first shifting to the right our aisle shifted just a little too hard to the left and sent a number of us to the floor. At the time we visited, they were still holding services in a small space, unlike the great space they have now. Unfortunately for us, the musicians didn't seem to care about the size of the room. Was it loud? Oy! Every time Karen and I looked at each other, our eyes got bigger and our hearing got smaller.

Even though it was nothing like what we've experienced before, we knew God was there. We've spent enough time in "proper" churches where no one falls on the floor and nothing powerful takes place, to know the real difference. This service may have been a little weird and unusual, but we could sure feel the presence of God.

Again, Cindy Jacobs happened to be speaking at this meeting. This time, thank God, we were over our desire for a dramatic prophetic word and were able to relax. No! Strike relax and replace with remain mostly stable, and listen.

Cindy spoke about what God was planning for Glory of Zion, Chuck Pierce's church and ministry. It was when she called for an offering that we knew this was our reason for being there. A couple of months earlier, God prompted us to start putting a little money away each week. We didn't know what it would be for, but we did it anyway. We had already used some for the t-shirts and necklaces. Now it was time to give, to plant some seed. Individually we had each planted seed, giving money to many ministries and people we each felt led to, but this would be the first time we gave together out of our business partnership. God always has a plan. Even if we can't figure it all out, we are determined to follow. And it wasn't just about giving the seed. We didn't know it yet, but God used Cindy Jacobs to connect us with Chuck Pierce and his ministry. We now know that God put him into our lives to help us walk in freedom. Besides that, you have to love a guy who's an apostle, prophet, *and* a bowler—and we do!

Chapter 7

A Kingdom Weekend

"I think we're supposed to go to New York," Karen said. "New York?" I smiled hoping it was true. She wasn't going to have to do any convincing, because I started mentally packing my bags before she even explained why.

We both had been having an unusual amount of dreams about our childhood home. We spent many nightly conversations discussing what could have been and what went wrong in our growing up years. We didn't grow up in a single parent or an abusive home, but even though we were all there together, you could say we were also all very much alone—all of us having our own issues. Looking back, it's easy to point out all the mistakes, but now things were different, we were different. Over the past year and a half, God had been doing some major renovation in us. We were no longer the unenlightened girls of our youth. A completely new foundation had to be built. At the same time as the building was progressing, demolition was also in full force. Demolition of all the old wrong mindsets had to be completely removed so that our new foundation would be solid, strong, and lasting. Our identities were being made new, but the past had so affected us, that we needed to physically go back to spiritually draw a line in the sand and declare that the past would no longer have any power over us.

We were calling this sudden field trip our "Kingdom weekend." The one thing we knew for sure that would be on our agenda, was that we would be going back to Long Island to rid ourselves from the negative roots of our past. We would be cursing the fig tree like Jesus did. We actually did have a real fig tree growing in the back yard of our childhood home. Karen was also bringing along her smooth giant killing stone that just happened to mysteriously appear in her car one day. We weren't coming back without victory. Fig tree cursing, root killing, enemy slaying, mountain moving, and taking the head off the giant. We planned on covering it all.

When it was time to make travel plans, it didn't take us very long to choose a hotel. As soon as we saw The New York Palace listed on a travel website—it was obvious. After all, where else would the King's daughters stay? On our own we could not have afforded to do this, but God had us begin to set money aside all those months ago. Some had gone toward our "I am Whosoever" t-shirts and pendants. Some was given as seed to Glory of Zion. And now, with the rest, God was sending us on a Kingdom adventure. Isn't God amazing?!

We arrived late on a Thursday evening. Coming into New York City at night, all lit up in that picture perfect way, like no other city, was so exciting. We confidently walked into The New York Palace Hotel feeling like total royalty. We were more than ready to experience all this trip would hold. Entering our room, we could almost hear a choir of angels sing as we pulled back the drapes and saw the breathtaking view of St Patrick's Cathedral. I think Karen heard that same angelic choir sing as she stepped into her plush pair of complimentary gold crested slippers while reaching for the elegantly wrapped chocolate resting on her pillow. "We're home. This is where we belong." We both laughed.

It didn't matter how tired we were or how late it

was, we had to get out and do something. After some midnight mid-town exploring, we found a late-night deli. With large hungry eyes we scanned the pastries, cheesecakes and bagels before choosing the perfect late night indulgence. We slept very well that night with full stomachs and dreams of a weekend filled with New York adventures. Early, well, our kind of early, the next morning we made our way to the nearest breakfast spot before picking up our rental car. We've separately spent time in the city on many other occasions, but this time everything felt so different. Partly because of our fancy hotel digs, partly because of the circumstances of this visit, but mostly because we always have so much fun together.

After breakfast, as we were walking down into the basement where our car would be found, Karen said, "*You* can drive." Even though I love to drive, I was just under the age of learning to drive when we left New York all those years ago, so this would be my first New York driving experience. Me! Driving in the city where even the best of drivers don't necessarily like to drive! Oy! As we stood in the tiny basement and I looked up at the extremely tight driveway of that car rental shop, I wondered if I could do this. Then, they brought us what appeared to be the longest widest sedan ever made.

"Yikes!" I screeched as I barely made it out of the driveway and onto a heavily crowded very narrow street. But then, as I turned onto the main avenue it was like I had just been let loose in the wild. It was as if I was playing a video game, and some idiot said, "Just drive as fast as you can and ignore the rest." Karen instinctively tightened her seat belt as I sped off trying to make it through as many green lights as possible without hitting any cabs or innocent pedestrians. Suddenly, it became very exciting. Karen said that it felt surreal, like she was in a movie and I was the stunt driver navigating the city in a highly choreographed manner. For me, IT WAS AWESOME! I felt strangely yet invigoratingly empowered in a way I've never felt before. I felt totally safe and in total control, even when I made a completely inconceivable u-turn in front of a huge truck to avoid missing the tunnel to the Island. Karen and I still marvel over that epic experience. Looking back now, I'm pretty sure there was an entire host of angels on assignment that day.

Once we made it out onto the Island and Karen was able to pry her fingers from the dashboard, our first stop was Richmond Hill. When we were planning our journey before we made this trip, Richmond Hill was not listed as one of our stops. Before our trip, Karen and I took a little shopping adventure in Dallas. We couldn't be going to New York City and not look good. While on our short shopping adventure, we drove up and down the North Dallas Tollway to get from store to store. The unusual part was that we would overshoot our exit and have to turn around and go back, every time we got off the tollway. We've both lived in Dallas and had driven up and down that road for many years. We were both a bit confused by what was happening. Karen said that it was happening to her as she was driving the day before as well. It felt a bit like a Twilight Zone episode. It was definitely weird, and like we often say, "If it's weird, it's God." We knew it had to be about our New York trip because that's why we were together that afternoon and that's what we were discussing in the car as we continuously passed by those exits. Later, on the way home, I specifically prayed, "God, are we going to miss a stop, a street, or an exit when we go to Long Island?" Instantly, Richmond Hill came to mind. I looked it up on the map when I got home. Yes! Karen and I both knew that this was the destination, the exit, we would have missed.

So, here we were in Richmond Hill. We parked on a quiet street in our old neighborhood. We talked a little about our memories as Karen began to write out a prayer of release. Karen said that this was the place where things began to turn in the wrong direction for her. She was once a happy little girl who used to conduct prayer meetings with her stuffed animals. Being the oldest of four, she was privy to too many family matters, and that innocent cheerful disposition became weighted down with worry. I, on the other hand, was only three years old, and was oblivious to all of it. But that doesn't mean that there was no affect on my life. The more we talked, the clearer it was to know exactly what to write, pray, and release. And it wasn't just about us and our own family, we were also praying for Uncle Jerry, another brother of our mom, and his family. He lived with us for a while during a difficult time in his life, and God put it on our hearts to add him and his family to this prayer of freedom. As we drove away, we could sense that a small yet heavy weight had been lifted.

After a short time of reflection and release, we were hungry. Unfortunately, everything makes *us* hungry. It was time to relive a *good* memory. So we headed straight for a Long Island diner, of course. We ordered all the yummy foods we thought we had been missing all our years living in Texas. We used to say, "I wish I could run to a Long Island diner and grab a cup of coffee and a cannoli or in my case, a coke and a big black and white cookie." Now here we were, but alas, the coffee was cold and the cookie was dry. Sadly, the memories were so much better than the real thing. We had no room for calories that weren't worth every bite, so we were off to our next adventure, battle, exorcism. I'm not sure what to call it, but we were off to accomplish it nevertheless.

We felt it was important to make the home of the fig tree, the one we so often dreamed of, our final mission. So we drove straight through that town where we would end our journey, and went directly to the last address we occupied as a family just before moving from New York.

As we drove into Freeport, our last place of family residence, neither of us could think of a good memory of living there. The weight of that place was intense. We could feel the heaviness and wanted to do what we needed to do and get out of there as quickly as possible. We felt we were never meant to live there, and only ended up there because of bad decisions. We could list the "if only's," but for what purpose? We were feeling a righteous anger over many wrong things we settled for, and with a warring determination, Karen wrote out our words of freedom and release. This would have been a good place to pull out our swords and violently wave them, cutting through the thickness, as we prayed and declared that we were free. Even though we may not have been wielding those physical swords, spiritually we were wielding the Word of God which is sharper than any two-edged sword.

Next, was Rockville Center. This was the big one. We made a quick stop at a convenient store to purchase some crackers and a small bottle of grape juice so that we could take communion at this important final destination. For us, taking communion is about more than just remembering all Jesus did for us, but also about receiving the healing and wholeness, and covering us with His blood.

This particular home, the one with the fig tree, held the most memories. It was where we lived during our formative teenage years. It was the place where so much of our wrong identities had been formed. After all these years, the house that once seemed so big, now looked so small. Even the very large tree that used to tower above our home was completely gone.

Here at our third and final location, we were getting pretty good at knowing exactly what to pray and declare. The prayer was written and communion taken. Then we looked up and down both sides of the street to make sure no one was coming before we got out of the car. We stood on the sidewalk next to where the large tree used to be. Karen held and read the pages as I reached for a match. We quickly knelt down, prayed, laid the pages on the ground, and set them ablaze as Karen placed her smooth giant killing stone on top. We watched until it was almost completely gone. It was finished.

For us, it wasn't just a symbolic act, it was much more. God had given us authority through the blood and in the name of Jesus. He taught us how to apply it and we did. We went back to the place where the root of a lot of unfruitfulness was planted and we cursed it and cut its head off. We would no longer be the girls we used to be. We declared that we were the new creation "Whosoevers" that God made us to be. And then we went to eat, because that's how we roll.

So, one last attempt at restoring the delicious diner memories of our past led us to yet another diner before making our way back to the city. After placing our order, we talked about how good it felt to do what needed to be done and how we would now be free to enjoy the city. Even though we couldn't physically feel a difference, we knew that spiritually something powerful had taken place.

"How's your food?" I asked. But her face really said it before she even got the words out, "not so great." Could it have been that we had lived in Texas so long that the BBQ, Tex-Mex, and chicken-fried steaks had won over our New York taste buds? Or maybe it was God just saying, "You're completely done here now, so move on." Either way, we were out of there.

Arriving back at The New York Palace, we sensed something was very different. Not just because of our new keen and intense senses, but primarily because of the many armed police officers and not-so-secret Secret Service now guarding our hotel. Maybe it was the ambulance and other emergency vehicles standing at-the-ready, or it could have been the giant blocks of cement blocking off parts of the streets that tipped us off. Even though we were feeling pretty important and special during this trip, we were pretty sure the grandeur wasn't for us. It appeared as if we were staying in either the safest or the most dangerous hotel in town. We could feel the vibe of a VIP in our midst as we made our way back to our room. We quickly got dressed to go out for a victory dinner and scope out the mystery. We were in New York, we had just cursed the fig tree and cut the head of a giant off, and now it was time to celebrate and enjoy the surroundings. Karen was even adorned with her giant golden scull of victory.

Weeks before this trip was even planned, Karen was strolling through the mall with her daughter when something large and gaudy caught her eye. A golden skull covered in diamond-like crystals. It was very big and very gold. The kind of bling that you might think only an over-the-top rap star could ap-preciate. To others it may have looked like just a skull, but to Karen it looked like a symbol of victory. She had been spending a lot of time slaying and cut-ting the heads off of many giants in her life. She wanted her medal, her trophy of victory. She didn't care if it did happen to set off the alarms of every place we went—she was proud of it.

Before we left the hotel for dinner, we had to know who or what was causing all this security fuss.

We tried the concierge and the front desk, but their lips were sealed. We walked out through the courtyard filled with trees covered in white twinkling lights, and made our way to the majestic front gates. We had to pass through an assembly of police and that's when Karen's big ole bling brought us secret access to answers. A high ranking officer complimented her choice of jewelry, and she in turn asked him for suggestions on where we might have dinner. Her gift of gab served her well as the secret was swiftly revealed. "A king!?" we both looked at each other extremely excited. Saudi Arabia's King Abdullah was in town, *in our hotel*, to meet with President George W. Bush, *in our hotel,* in just a few days. This was big. God placed us there, in that very hotel, with a king, for such a time as this. We were expecting some awesome things to happen this weekend, but this was more than we imagined. Immediately, we knew that we were there for more than an autograph.

As we sat down for dinner at the fancy restaurant suggested by our new bling-admiring police friend, we couldn't really concentrate on anything else. It was discernible to us that God was entrusting us to fulfill more than one mission that weekend. God was commissioning us with a major assignment: To pray.

It was our Kingdom assignment to pray for the safety of both the King and our President. To pray for God's blessing, peace, and protection to cover Israel.

To pray that *God's* agenda be accomplished when these two powerful men would meet in just a few days, and also during the UN meetings to follow.

When we got back to our hotel, which now was truly "The Palace," we spent that night praying some, but mostly talking about how cool God is. The next morning we got to work: We prayed in our room, in the elevators, and at each entrance to the hotel. Then we went to eat, because if you didn't catch it already, that's how we do it. We headed out the south entrance to walk toward Park Avenue. As soon as we stepped outside we were standing in the midst of many SWAT-like officers with very big guns. I felt as if I'd just walked onto a movie set. I wanted to take a picture with them to show my kids, but Karen grabbed my arm because she has this funny rule: if you see men with machine guns, it's best to keep moving.

We were walking up the street completely over-taken by a fleet of big black Mercedes. When the King travels, he brings along a sizable entourage of princes, security people and personal attendants, as well as all their own resources, including linens, dishes, silver etc.. There's a pretty good analogy to the Kingdom of God in that sentence, and though I feel a sermon coming on, hard as it may be, I'll let it go and hope you can figure it out for yourself. Back to the earthly King, we realized that we were the only non-security people standing on that particular street. When we passed by a curtained off back door, we could see that they were preparing for the King to come out. We didn't get to actually see him, but just standing in the midst of all that hubbub was impressive.

We spent most of that day doing a little sightseeing and a lot of shopping. While strolling down Park Avenue between our hotel and The Waldorf-Astoria, another luxury hotel filled with more Saudi princes, we passed by a number of K-9 officers. Karen asked me if I had noticed the odd way each of those big German shepherds had tilted their heads and stared at us. But before I could suggest that it might be her bacon scented perfume, she said, "I believe they can see angels walking with us." I couldn't help but think she was right realizing that we *were* the only ones those big pups seemed to take notice of. Our weekend seemed to be filled with many curious moments that filled us with a sense of wonder.

That night, our final night, we went to Times Square to complete our third and final New York mission. Remember those "I Am Whosoever" necklace pendants we made months earlier? They turned out to be seeds. Let me explain: They are small and oval shaped, and embossed on one side is "I Am Whosoever," and on the other side "John 3:16", "John 4:14", and "Mark 11:23."

In case you don't know... John 3:16 says, *"For God so loved the world, that He gave His only begotten Son, that Whosoever believeth in Him should not perish, but have everlasting life."* John 4:14 says, *"Whosoever drinketh of the water that I shall give him shall never thirst; but the water that I shall give him shall be in him a well of water springing up into everlasting life."* And Mark 11:23 says, *"Whosoever shall say unto this mountain, Be thou removed, and be thou cast into the sea; and shall not doubt in his heart, but shall believe that those things which he saith shall come to pass; he shall have whatsoever he saith."*

The details of the how and the why we were literally meant to plant some of these in the ground as seed is a long story still to be completed. What I can say is that we had planted our first seed in Texas. We planted it in Austin, the capital of Texas, near the foot of the tower of The University of Texas. The University that proudly declares, "What starts here changes the world."

So now, here we were in Times Square, New York City, and about to plant another seed. If you've ever been there, you're probably wondering where we could possibly find a place to plant something in a concrete jungle—so were we. But then, we noticed we were standing in front of a drainage grate on the edge of the street. So we prayed over it, and yes, we dropped it right into that grate; right in the location where two and a half years later a car bomb meant to destroy Times Square failed. Coincidence? Not when God's involved. We're just telling—you decide.

The entire weekend had been a great whirlwind of emotional and exciting adventures that far exceeded our expectation. We couldn't wait to get home and see what would happen next. We felt ready to take on the world.

Chapter 8

The Assignment

It was almost Thanksgiving when we returned from New York. We kept the details of our very personal Long Island mission to ourselves, but when we tried to share the excitement of the King and all the rest with our family, they weren't as excited as we were.

The holidays kept us busy, so we assumed the "running the world" part would probably begin in January. On January 1st through the 4th we attended another Glory of Zion event. It was called *Starting The Year Off Right*, and it did start our year off right. A lot of our favorite people were there: Cindy Jacobs, Judy Jacobs, Dutch Sheets, Alan Vincent, Keith

Miller, Barbara Wentroble, Chuck Pierce, of course, and others. They may not have known us, but we had read their books, we knew their amazing testimonies, and we felt like we were part of their tribe. For us, it was like a pep rally moving us forward into the new year. We didn't know then that there would be little pep and no rallies for quite some time after that.

We waited for something to happen. We expected God to tell us that it was time to set up a business. Karen wanted and needed financial blessings to start flowing. We both expected to walk straight into our destiny, but that didn't happen. It appeared that our "special order" still wasn't ready. "God, we don't understand," we cried. "How could you give us such an amazing taste of Kingdom living, and then nothing?"

After weeks of having such momentum, and walking on a victorious high, we hit a low point. We felt like kids who had to go back to school after some great weeks of Christmas vacation. We had to hold each other up and remind ourselves of all that God had taught us over the past two years of training. We thought we had graduated, and maybe we had, but there is always a next level—more, much more to learn.

This wasn't our first low moment. Always trying to presume what was to come next continually messed us up. We clearly hadn't mastered the art of resting in God's timing yet. In between every exciting moment that took place there were quite a few discouraging times of whining and wondering if we would ever reach our place of destiny. Thank God we didn't go through those short yet painful periods at the same time. When one of us was having an off day or more like a week or three, the other would say, "You know what to do. Get your Bible out and start saying what God says" or "Go get alone with God!" This undeniably correct advice usually doesn't go over so well when you're in a doubting and weary of waiting mood. What you really want is the stuff, the check, the job, the blessing to just be handed over. Fortunately, the "you know what to do" speech was always given by phone and neither of us had to feel the slap that the other was ready to dish-out upon hearing annoyingly correct, but not so much wanted, advice.

Thankfully, after we had our pity parties, we always returned to the meeting place, the place of renewing. Spending time one-to-One with God never fails to bring us right back into alignment. And as time went on, those times of discouragement would grow shorter and way less frequent.

Now, as we look back on that time, coming back from New York, foolishly thinking we were ready to conquer the world, we are *very* thankful that we didn't get our wish. We can see God's pattern. How it was all part of the process, the plan God had to get us from who we were to who we are now.

We may not have been ready to conquer the world yet, but God did give us a new assignment. For a long time, we had been talking about writing a book—several books really. Even though there was still more to learn, as there always is, we had already gained so much valuable knowledge, and we wanted to share it. Before God got a hold of us, we joked about writing a funny drive-thru-therapy style book, but Karen had no patience for idiotic behavior and just wanted to physically slap people into wisdom. When anything unusual happens to us, I always say, that will make a good chapter. I actually did write some stories about our couple of months of being interior designers and then jewelry makers and designers and then home furnishings manufacturers and designers etc..., but while those stories were quite funny and had us continually amused, they didn't end in success.

So now, all along our new journey we would say, people need to know this stuff; we really need to write a book. Though we discussed it often, this was the first time that we felt we were finally ready to say something valuable. We knew *what* we were supposed to write about, we just weren't sure if it was the right time.

It would be the book that would have helped us when we were younger; the book Karen wished she'd read when she had cancer. It would be the book we wanted to hand our friends, and the book we wanted our children to read. We felt the weight and importance of such a book, but we needed God's go ahead before we would get started. In the past we had done so many things out of God's timing and so we were very concerned with getting it right this time. It seemed like the right time, but God would have to confirm it.

When God had us focused on learning all about the Kingdom, we read Bill Johnson's book *When Heaven Invades Earth*. After that I would often watch videos of worship and sermons on his website. A lot of awesome things happen in his church and our faith and awe always grows as we hear the many inspiring and often jaw dropping testimonies of what God is doing. We first read his book because Karen had heard Evangelist Marilyn Hickey, speak about how good it was, and how it had changed *her* life. Karen then called and told me about it. She said she wasn't sure of the author's name, just that it was something weird or unusual. I called her from the book store and said, "Weird like—Bill? Like—Bill Johnson?" It's a good thing she gave me the title or I may never have found it.

Searching Bill's Bethel Church website one day, I

noticed on his itinerary that he would be speaking at a church only a few miles away. Karen and I, never giving up a chance to get out, quickly made arrangements to be there. Bill Johnson knew what it meant to have a Kingdom mindset, and we knew that he was a guy diligently pursuing more of God. Through his teaching and writing we learned the truth about what "on earth as it is in heaven" meant. This guy was living on a level of faith that we wanted to attain. We were excited and expectant as we went to hear him speak that night. As expected, the teaching was great, but the best, most exciting part was when he, Bill Johnson, stopped and said, "This is for someone here, God says, Write that book!" Wow! We looked at each other with wide eyes and mouths agape, and quickly both declared, "THAT'S FOR US!" As you can imagine, we were so excited driving home that night. We immediately began to make plans to begin writing. We decided that we would meet each week on a Sunday afternoon.

It was thrilling to finally begin working on a project. That first Sunday we met up at a little cafe halfway between our two homes. Finally, we had the wisdom to combine the assignment and the crucial eating part into one destination. We ordered some soup and sandwiches, found the most comfortable booth, and began writing an outline.

There were so many things that we wanted to

cover in the book. It would be about identity, about becoming the Whosoevers written about in the Bible. Starting with "Whosoever believes" and ending with "Whosoever says" to the mountain, be thou removed. It would be about knowing what it means to have a two-way conversation with an awesome God who is closer than you think. It was to be about everything that made us say, "This is powerful. Why didn't we know this?"

First, we wrote out an introduction. It was good, and had us both stating, "I want to read this book." Not good because *we* were such brilliant writers, but good because it was clearly words that *only* the Holy Spirit could have inspired through us. The ease of the introduction, and beginning outline, had us foolishly thinking, "This book could be finished in just a few weeks."

We wanted to write about the details, beyond forgiveness and going to Heaven someday, of all that the blood of Jesus purchased for us: about being set free and what it means to be in right-standing with God, about abundance, health, wealth, gaining wisdom, knowledge, understanding, and revelation, about how to build a strong foundation, and how Jesus has already done all of it, everything. He has already given us the victory we're always crying out for, and we just need to believe it, receive it and enforce it. Like we said, so much to write about. And yes, we can back it all up with scripture.

The details of the new identity Jesus died to give us would be the main focus of the book, and it had to be thorough. We also had to write about the battle, about the unseen but very real spiritual battle going on all around us, about how satan's highest goal is to steal worship from God; about how he tries to keep us from going to the meeting place, the place where we meet God one-to-One. All of this would mean we'd better get it right. We'd better do a lot of praying and some serious Bible studying. Studying had never been one of our strongest traits, but that was about to change. God *is* a miracle worker.

We dove through our Bibles, searched our concordances, and expanded our libraries. The more we studied and wrote the more *we* were learning. As we reviewed and wrote out all that we had been taught over the previous couple of years, we were able to see it from a new perspective and receive a deeper understanding.

Then we realized that something we didn't expect was happening. The book that started out one way was becoming more of a teaching, and less of the intimate conversation we wanted to have with the reader. We became confused and started to wonder if this writing process was really about *us* and less about an actual book. Were we really writing a book or was God just cleverly putting us through some kind of graduate school? It was confusing because we knew we had something important to say, and we weren't quite sure how to fix it. We were missing the stories, the real life experiences that help us to see how we can apply the teaching, the message, in our own lives. We would often talk about how the real life stories, in the many books we read, were the parts that effected us the most. They were what we remembered and what spoke most loudly to us. We just didn't think our own stories were important enough.

Chapter 9

Time To Roar!

It was Christmas time *again*, and *yes*, many months past the three weeks we thought it might take to write the book. Instead of taking our own advice to press in and seek out an answer on how we should proceed, we took a break. We weren't enjoying the time off from writing. We were so sure that the book was going to be the beginning of our promised future, and we were starting to get a little stir crazy. And even if we wanted to get together again to continue writing, we couldn't. Karen's car was no longer running and the bank accounts were mighty low.

And then, Hallelujah! Yet another free event came

up that gave us something to look forward to. Mahesh Chavda, a miracle-working man of God, was going to be speaking and we knew it would be worth attending. This guy had not only been places, but he had seen and done so many exciting and powerful things. God had given him a big life filled with a special anointing and we wanted some of it to touch us.

Just as we expected, he carried a powerful message that ignited a new fight in us. He spoke mainly about the glory of God: about what it's like operating in the realm of God's glory, and about how miracles take place in the glory. The glory realm is when the presence of God invades the atmosphere; it's what the atmosphere of Heaven is made up of. He told us a few stories of great miracles, but my favorite was when he was at an event in India.

A young girl had brought her blind grandmother up for healing. Mahesh said that he prayed, but she was still blind. The next night of this event, again the girl brought her grandmother up for prayer, but still she remained blind. For seven nights the grandmother got in line and received prayer. On the seventh and final night, Mahesh quickly prayed for her and moved on to the next person. As he began to pray for others, he heard a commotion and realized that the little girl's grandmother could suddenly see. She was completely healed. Why did it take the seven nights? Mahesh didn't really know until some time later when God gave him a vision of what took place. He said that he could see a thing looking like an octopus, a demonic-spirit over that woman's eyes. Every night as he prayed for her, one tentacle or octopus leg would peel off of her eyes. Finally, on the seventh night, the last remaining tentacle was peeled off and she was free. She could see.

Just as so many other stories help us to have a picture of what's taking place in the spirit realm all around us, this one helps us to remember to be persistent and relentless in prayer. Because even though we might not be able to see something happening with our natural eyes, something *is* taking place in the spirit realm.

Mahesh also spoke about joy that night. Then he took it a little further by asking God to fill those who needed some joy with a supernatural touch of joy. He asked everyone to place their hand over their belly as he prayed for a release of joy. All of a sudden, Karen began to laugh along with several others. She seemed to be surprised by her own laughter and couldn't stop it. At first, I wanted to pretend I wasn't with her as she giggled uncontrollably. But then, the laughter became contagious as the rest of us began to laugh along with them. It was kind of weird, but cool at the same time. Even later, while Karen and I were having dinner, anytime she thought about it, she would again begin to involuntarily laugh. She kept saying,

"It's not me. I can't stop it." It was a pretty potent dose of joy because she laughed off and on the rest of that night. At the time, she was definitely in need of joy and was happy to receive it. I sometimes had to laugh just because she couldn't stop, but my laughter was controllable and I was sort of jealous.

Later, Mahesh began to pray for specific people in the audience. Though I can't remember exactly what he said, I do remember nudging Karen and saying, "Go! That's you he's speaking to."

As she stepped forward into the prayer lineup of about 12 people, she noticed that as Mahesh laid his hand on each person they fell back and were now lying on the floor. She was determined to stay standing, and was pretty sure he had sort of pushed them as they willingly fell back. Just in case you're wondering, there were people behind catching them so none were injured. When Mahesh reached Karen, he stopped, prayed, and just slightly blew on her like he was blowing out a tiny candle. Before she could even comprehend what was happening, she found herself lying on the ground along with the others.

Needless to say, we had a whole lot to discuss over the dinner break. I was asking questions that she couldn't answer. "What was that? How did it happen? What did you feel? What happened when you were on the floor?" She said that she couldn't stop it, but wasn't sure about what exactly had happened. She remembered that she couldn't move. She felt paralyzed and wasn't even aware of how long she may have been laying down there. She got up as soon as she was able. And no, she didn't have a vision or encounter while on the floor, but she knew that something powerful definitely happened. For her, the most unusual thing was that Mahesh touched the others, but not her. He merely blew on her. Had God caused him to do that because she had a bit of a skeptical attitude? I warned her about her list of nevers.

Also at this conference, Joann Mcfatter, a singer, songwriter, and teacher, taught how science was just beginning to catch up with the Bible: About sound, and what scientific studies have discovered about what happens when we speak positive or negative words out-loud. She spoke about the many ways science and the Bible actually align. Who knew that you could go to a prayer and worship gathering and get a lesson on quantum physics? I had always been saying, maybe sometimes whining, that I wanted to know more details. I wanted to know the why and the how things work. That's why I loved hearing Mahesh tell the story of how God had shown him what was happening in the spirit realm as he prayed in the natural. I was excited to be getting some answers, some inspiring details of the interaction between the seen and unseen realm. It was very interesting and informative. It not only gave us deeper insight into the power of speaking God's Word outloud, but also greatly expanded our perspective. You gotta love when God does that.

It seems God brought us to this meeting to, yet again, expand our vision. To open us up to all He's doing and remind us to expect more and not ever limit what God can and will do.

But the meeting wasn't over yet. Mahesh spoke again the next morning. This time he told us about an encounter he once had with a lion. He spoke about the powerful and authoritative roar of a lion, and likened it to the kind of authority we have through the blood and in the name of Jesus. Eventually, he even had us all loudly roaring like lions. Normally, I would have just pretended to roar like I used to pretend to sing in elementary school choir, but God was doing something in us and I wasn't about to miss out on any of it. A supernatural boldness told my pride to shut up and roar! It reminded me of when Karen and I went to that first meeting in Waco. It was the first time that she and I had been in church *together* since we began this journey. Though I don't remember the exact song that we were singing, what I do remember was sensing such a strong presence of God. I wanted to raise my hands in worship, but a mixture of shyness, pride, and my sister standing next to me had me hesitating. Finally, the overwhelming desire to freely worship won over, and I began to cry as I lifted my hands high. Even now, thinking back on that moment brings tears to my eyes. Words can't really explain the freedom it brought me. First lifting my hands, and now roaring—what's next?

Later, in the evening session, Keith Miller of Stand Firm World Ministries, spoke about receiving the supernatural wisdom of God. He told us that God wants to impart that wisdom into each and every one of us if we're willing. Karen and I had read Keith's book *Surrender to the Spirit,* and remembered the story about how he had once been hired to handle a big job he wasn't really equipped to handle. God gave him a dream showing him very precise details of what needed to be done. Because of that supernatural wisdom, his business grew overnight.

Over the past few years of learning and growing, we had heard many exciting stories of how a download of God's wisdom had completely changed people's lives; from getting daily directions, songs, books, or inventions, to receiving words of knowledge, and specific strategies and words to pray or say. In the Bible, there are many great stories of God-given wisdom, from Noah's ark to the wisdom Paul operated in. Hearing about how God's imparting wisdom *still* today, in so many amazing and very detailed ways, is truly inspiring.

But wait, there's more. At the end of that session there was still a fire tunnel to go through. Yes, you read that right, a "fire tunnel." It sounds weird but really isn't as weird as you might think. The leaders and prayer team formed two rows facing each other, while everyone else lined up and quickly walked through the tunnel of praying leaders who laid hands on each of us. It wasn't just random prayer that they prayed over us. They prayed for an impartation of wisdom, knowledge, and revelation, and of course—joy.

After a weekend filled with great worship and teaching, we were willing to go the distance. So, we didn't sneak out as we may have in our past years. It became pretty clear to us that the power of the Holy Spirit was in that fire tunnel because we noticed some people hitting the floor just before making it to the entrance. Karen had already had her moment on the ground the day before, but I didn't know what to expect. She pushed me in front so I had to go first. I closed my eyes, not because I was scared, but because that's what I do when someone prays. I could hear people praying and feel people touching my back and shoulders as I went through. Then I could feel someone on either side holding me up because I could no longer stand on my own. That's when Keith Miller touched me and said, "more Lord." I began to involuntarily laugh as he kept saying, "more Lord more." The more he said "more" the more I laughed. As I was finally lifted up and pushed out of the line, I almost lost my balance and nearly knocked over the people in front of me. That's when I looked back and saw them dragging Karen out of the middle of the fire tunnel by her feet.

Neither of us could stop laughing as we got our stuff and made our way to the car. Apparently, she only made it a few steps into the tunnel before she was out. The moment was over, but the vision of me being pushed from the line, and Karen being dragged out by her feet, still makes us laugh. If you think these events are a bit strange, we suggest you read the strange things God had the biblical prophets do!

Clearly, God has a sense of humor. Even though we laugh over this unusual experience, something *did* happen in that tunnel. It may not have been visible to our natural eyes, but we *know* we received something great that weekend. And it seems God also used that weekend to knock some old religious walls down that had been built around us. We would no longer limit God. What was once so weird and unusual had now become our normal. Our old pride, judgement, and skepticism had all been surrendered, and because of it, we were free to receive what we once may have rejected. God kept leading the way and we were always willing to follow.

Chapter 10

Tragedy And Triumph

In the beginning of May, four months after setting the book down, Karen and I were about to attend another event. This one came without warning and was sadly unexpected. We were on our way to a funeral home in Lindale, Texas. Just days earlier, the headlines read, "Rev. David Wilkerson Dies in a Head-on Collision." Uncle Dave was gone in a sudden and very tragic accident.

For so long we had tried to pull away from the Wilkerson connection. We weren't interested in running or being involved in a ministry. We didn't want to be in "the family business"—that whole idea of riding on the coattails thing. We believed our calling was different. But, as you can see from our story, God wouldn't let us set the whole bloodline family connection aside. The more we grew and began walking in our new identity, the less we tried to pull away from the heritage that helped us to stand where we now were.

We had finally realized that it wasn't really a family thing after all, it was a God thing. Because of the prayers that had gone before, Uncle Dave reached out for more. And when God answered with a call, Uncle Dave said, "Yes!" And now, because of what had gone before us, we too were reaching, hearing God, and answering that call with a great big "Yes!"

As we made our way toward Lindale, Karen remembered a rare moment she shared with Uncle Dave on her seventh birthday. She was invited to stay for a week at his home with our cousins Debi, Bonnie, and Gary. Uncle Dave put all the kids into his convertible and took them to the store. Karen started to laugh, as she remembered how her seven year old mind was very concerned for Uncle Dave's salvation when he turned on the radio and began to sing "The Monster Mash." She was pretty sure that only a sinner could possibly know all the words to a song like that. When they arrived at the store, Uncle

Dave told Karen to pick out any bicycle she wanted. The best part of Karen's memory was that Uncle Dave actually took the time to teach her how to ride her first bicycle. She can still see him happily running up and down that dead end street, holding onto the side of her bicycle, until she was able to balance herself. I was surprised to hear that story, and wished I could have known *that* Uncle Dave, but my moments with him were different and way less personal. The one thing Karen and I did both share was a deep respect for Uncle Dave's calling.

Even though we knew that the mantle, the calling, on the Wilkerson bloodline, began generations before Uncle Dave, we knew that whatever the exact and specific "thing" God called on this family to accomplish was *on* him. And for that reason, Karen and I often talked about how the next time we were in the Lindale area, we would go to Twin Oaks. Twin Oaks is the original land Uncle Dave purchased and operated his ministry from, and the land where he so often walked and talked to God. We had read and heard many stories of how a tangible presence, anointing, whatever you want to call it, sometimes remains on a place. We wanted to go back there and get it—not his ministry or his specific calling, but the "thing." We wanted that particular something that God intended for our family.

We took the scenic route to the funeral home so

that we could drive onto that land. Another ministry now owned the land, and no one was at the front gate so we drove on through. Karen had been there in the late 1970s and tried to point out where she remembered Uncle Dave walking, but everything looked different all these years later. As we stopped the car and sat for a moment trying to figure out what to do and where to go, Karen suddenly said, "I know what it is. You've been saying it all along." "What...what is?" I asked. "The thing!" she said. "It's prayer!" she declared. That's what this family has, that's what Uncle Dave did as he walked, that's what our grandfather did, and his mother before him. That is the power that this family holds and the very reason for the success of Teen Challenge and the rest, it's about the power of prayer. Our family has a call to be a fervent praying force, if only we are willing and choose to respond. She began to cry as my heart began to beat faster, "Yes! It's about prayer!"

I remember how nearly two years earlier, I had heard a minister speak about why we *have to* pray. Because God gave the earth to man, we have to ask him to intervene in our affairs, otherwise He won't. It was another one of those "aha" moments, but I also wondered if it could really be true. I remember praying, "God, is this right? Please show me." He did, and more importantly, it is! Karen and I always make sure we ask God to confirm anything and everything we learn through His Word. What convinced me most about why we must pray, was Ezekiel 22:30-31 where God says, "*I sought for a man among them, that should make up the hedge, and stand in the gap before Me for the land, so that I should not destroy it; but I found none.*" John Wesley, co-founder of the Methodist Church, once said, "God does nothing but in answer to prayer." This opened my eyes in a new way. Prayer is not just important, it's essential!

When we arrived at the funeral home, we were happy to see Greg, Uncle Dave's youngest son, one of the cousins for whom we had so fervently been praying for a very long time. For several years he had been suffering from a debilitating back injury, but now he looked like a new person. He was completely healed and walked and talked with a spirit of joy. It was great to know that Uncle Dave had lived long enough to see Greg's healing manifest. A few months before Greg's healing, Karen sent Greg and his wife prayer ladened "I am Whosoever" necklaces. When Teresa, Greg's wife, was introduced to Karen at the funeral, she thanked Karen and said that she had felt something special on those necklaces. God was using us, because we were willing to respond to Him, in ways that never ceased to surprise us.

The family gathering would be like none we had experienced before. This time we were different. When we arrived, we weren't Wilkersons, Harris',

Lindqvists, or Drevermanns, we were daughters of the King. We were finally truly walking in our rightful identity. It was a day that, for us, would bring forgiveness and restoration in ways that only God could accomplish.

The service was inspiring. As we listened to the many moving stories and memories others shared about our uncle, we were awestruck by the details of what he had accomplished on his journey with God. The one constant thread that ran through all their testimonials, was prayer. They all recounted how often they remembered him going off alone to pray. Unexpected tears came to our eyes as the heart of the man, we only really knew as Uncle Dave, was revealed. The tears turned into worship as Dallas Holm began to sing "Here we are in Your presence lifting holy hands to You. Here we are praising Jesus for the things He's brought us through." It was a song we memorized and sang so often in our youth. Uncle Dave is gone, but we know without a doubt that the legacy of prayer that he so faithfully valued and carried on would continue to go on.

After the funeral, something was different, we were different. We had graduated to a new level. Our confidence had grown and we felt empowered in a new way. We still had plenty of battles to fight, and even though they looked pretty big, we knew the victory was already ours.

We again, renewed our commitment and time with God. We say, again, because keeping the commitment, staying in that place of continual prayer and worship is often a battle. Daily life, the world, job, family, friends, television, etc...wages a constant battle for our attention. Just as in the beginning of this journey, we have to continuously purpose to keep our daily appointment with God. Because when we don't, things gradually become grey, confused, and basically—not good.

We were stronger and fervently praying, but still we wondered, where was the rest of the assignment? As we prayed and pondered over this question, God began to open our eyes to where we'd messed up. Yes! Yikes! Oy! all of that stuff, we missed something along the way. God didn't tell us that we were finished with the book. He did tell us to "write that book!" but there was no word to stop writing. When the writing became difficult and a little confusing, we made up our own story of why we were supposed to stop. In our "aha" revelation and repentance, God showed us that the book, the first book we were to write, was our story. And that's when we began to write this book.

In the writing, we were able to see that the real gift God gave us wasn't the stuff, the physical blessing we kept looking to receive, but the identity. The gift is that we are the free and empowered overcoming "Whosoevers" He designed us to be. While we will always be a work in progress, we are completely different from the girls who began this walk more than five years ago. Fear, worry, and feeling powerless is gone, and in its place is a growing faith, an almost unexplainable peace, an emboldened confidence, and a great anticipation of a promised exciting and abundant future.

Chapter 11

Walking With Authority

We were different, and we were not just feeling it, we were seeing things happen. The city began a major renovation in the park behind my home. New pathways, new playground equipment, new benches and basketball hoops were coming to our park. A neighbor said, "This is weird, I've been living on this park for many years, and the city usually just re-paints the old equipment and nothing more." As Karen and I discussed all that was happening, it became clear.

Since the day we moved here, I've been out walking and praying in that park almost daily. I knew all those kids by name and they knew me. Karen said, "Laurie, that park and those kids are your assignment. It's your place of influence and authority." I knew she was right.

Now I was prayer-walking that park with a higher purpose. I began to pray for each child by name, for the neighborhood, and even the land. I believe that the park renovation was God showing me the fruit of all my past prayer, and it gave me the faith and momentum to fervently pray that every one of my park kids would become Kingdom kids. *They* were my real assignment.

After the new concrete pathways had been poured, I wished that I had thought about planting some Bible verses under it. Then, just a day or two later, I noticed that four small sections of the new pathway were being torn up. They said it was because the concrete had not been poured correctly in those sections, but I believed it happened just for me. The night before they were to re-pour new concrete, my older son and I ran out to the park so that I could bury those verses. I actually used complete pages that I removed from an old Bible. As I planted the book of Matthew in one section, Mark in another, and Luke and John in the final two sections, I prayed that God's Word would go out and do exactly what he plans, just like it says in Isaiah 55:11. I had read many stories of how people had completed prophetic acts like this, and I knew that this covert mission was a very meaningful event.

It wasn't the only prophetic act made in that park. I had been having one of those "God is trying to tell me something" moments. Again, the 222 thing was happening. It was everywhere I looked. Finally one morning, as I was checking my e-mails—Yikes! I had so many. But wait, it was exactly 222. "Okay God, what?" I mumbled to myself as I opened e-mail number 222. It was only an ad for a restaurant called Morton's, but then—wait, the address of Morton's was 2222 McKinney Ave. I didn't figure it all out right away, but later that day I received a mailing telling us about an environmental group that was working on getting rid of a battery plant not far from our park. Apparently, years of operation had released toxic chemicals into the environment. I was a bit upset. I knew God brought us to this place, but now, I was hearing about this poison nearby. "What am I to do, God?" I asked. I knew I needed some direction, a prayer to pray, a strategy. It wasn't until I was sitting in the local library with my children, when all of a sudden, I said out-loud, "Morton!—Salt!" Immediately, I remembered how I had read about a group that had gone somewhere to pray over the land and the people. I read about how they prophetically poured salt into the water and prayed that God would clean and purify the environment. The creek that runs through our park also runs through the battery plant site. The water runs from our park down through another neighborhood and eventually through the land the plant was sitting on. I asked God for a plan and He gave me one.

When I got home, I put some salt into a cup, prayed a quick prayer and walked to the place where the water first enters the park. I hoped no one saw me as I threw the salt into the creek. But alas, the salt blew right back into my direction instead of into the creek. Oy! Okay, obviously I'm not doing this right, I thought as I went back home. This time, I prayed and then looked up Biblical salt references. Salt is mentioned 40 times in the King James version of the Bible. There was even a salt covenant. I read that salt is meant to heal, purify, and create a thirst. So this time, I added water to the cup, and declared, "In Jesus name, the act of salting the water will heal, purify, and create a thirst for Jesus," as I successfully tossed the salt into the creek. Just a few weeks later, to the surprise of many, including me, it was announced that the battery plant would be closing.

As you can imagine, I was pretty excited to hear that news. I prayer-walked that park with great authority after that. I prayed, "Kingdom come and will of God be done." I prayed for peace, for healing, for blessing, but mostly that God's light would shine in that park. Several weeks after continuously praying for "the light," just as when I was praying for my spiritual inheritance and received "George" (a physical inheritance), literal lights were unexpectedly added to the park. Again, I knew I was seeing a physical manifestation of what was happening spiritually. I love when God does that.

The list of kids that I prayed for kept getting longer. I would sometimes sit in the park and read while my boys played with their friends. New kids would often come sit by me and tell me their names and even unknowingly give specific details that I knew God wanted me to pray about. I knew that bigger assignments and responsibilities would eventually come my way, but this park and these kids would be the place where I would learn how to operate in Kingdom authority. Zachariah 4:10 says, *"Do not despise these small beginnings, for the LORD rejoices to see the work begin..."*

As my small beginning was in progress, Karen was also seeing things happen. Someone had gifted Karen $100. She began to think about all the possible ways she might spend that money. She could buy a new pair of shoes, go for a great steak dinner, or maybe even just do like our kids would want to do when they were younger—spend it all at the Dollar Store. God had other plans. She did go to a dollar store, but not to buy 100 things; instead, God prompted her to give it to Loretta. Loretta was the older woman at the cash register that would often chitchat with Karen. Karen simply said, "I felt God tell me to give you this" as she folded it up and slipped it to her in between customers.

Karen felt that what she had just done was important. When she got into the car after giving that money to Loretta she could hear the sound of rushing water and asked her husband if he was hearing it too. He didn't, but that didn't matter because she knew that a breakthrough moment had just occurred. The odd thing was that Karen saw Loretta several times after that, and Loretta never said a word about it.

Weeks later, as Karen was on her way back to that same dollar store for some laundry detergent, she began to cry and say, "God, can I really hear you?" She wiped her tears, went into the store, got her detergent, and stepped into the line. Loretta happened to be working that night. This time when she saw Karen, she thanked her for the money and said, "Because of that money, I was able to go see my mom in Louisiana one last time before she died." Karen again began to get teary eyed as she told Loretta about how she had wondered if she actually had heard God. Loretta said, "You heard God!"

Not too long after that, on another shop-and-chat

visit, Loretta complained of having a bad migraine headache. Before she could even think, Karen boldly grabbed her hand and began to pray for Loretta—with authority, right there in that busy line. It was the first time Karen had prayed for someone so publicly and with such boldness. On a later visit, she heard Loretta yelling to her from across the store, "It worked! It worked! Your prayer worked!" she loudly shouted without caring who heard. Loretta told Karen that after she prayed for her that day, the migraine was totally gone. She said, "I was 100% healed!"

That wasn't Karen's only retail store miracle either. While in line in the grocery store one afternoon, she heard the grocery store manager telling someone that she had lost her wedding rings. Karen asked about the details of how she lost them. She was told that it happened at a restaurant. The grocery manager had gone into the ladies' room where she took off her rings and set them on the counter while she washed her hands. It wasn't until she was sitting back at her table that she remembered leaving them on the counter. She ran back into the ladies' room, but they were gone. Karen said, "I'm going to pray that you get those rings back." The grocery manager said, "Oh, those rings are long gone," as she waved off the possibility of reclaiming them. Karen felt God prompting her to pray—so she did. She prayed that those rings would be returned. A few days later, Karen noticed that the grocery manager was wearing those rings. She told Karen that she had gone to eat in that restaurant again, and noticed that her waitress was wearing *her* rings. When confronted, the waitress admitted to taking them and had to give them back to the rightful owner. Just as Karen had prayed, the rings *were* returned.

While it may sound like it (*and please don't tell her husband*) Karen doesn't actually have to go shopping to see answers to prayer. At another powerful conference we attended, Karen picked up a couple of prayer laden cloths. If you think prayer cloths sound a bit weird, so did Karen, but in Acts 19:11-12 the Bible says, *"God did extraordinary miracles through Paul; so that even handkerchiefs and aprons that had touched him were taken to the sick, and their illnesses were cured and the evil spirits left them."* Karen added her own prayer, and then gave one of those cloths to her husband, Paul, and the other to her son, Andrew. They each put them into the glove compartments of their trucks. Yes, we're fully Texans now, and Texans drive big-ole pickup trucks—it's an unwritten law.

A couple of days later, both Paul and Andrew were saved from what could have been very serious accidents. Paul was pulling a fully loaded trailer behind his truck. When he stopped at a light, he saw that loaded trailer drive right past him. It sounds a bit humorous now, but when Paul saw it go across the median and head straight for a gas station fuel pump—he wasn't laughing. The miracle was that it stopped just inches away from colliding into that fuel pump. Paul was shaken, but not harmed. Witnesses to the event quickly got out of their cars and helped Paul get that trailer right back onto his truck as if nothing had happened.

On the very same day, Andrew was nearly t-boned by a driver who ran a stop sign. He's not sure about how he managed to get out of the way, but simply said, "Mom, it was weird." They knew it wasn't "the cloth" that saved them, but wholly believed that it was the prayer those cloths were laden (fully-charged) with that protected them.

In Matthew 10:8, we're called to *"heal the sick, raise the dead, and cast out demons."* just as Jesus did, and taught his followers to do as well. We may not have been raising the dead—yet, but I know I was definitely casting out some demons from that park, and Karen was certainly out healing the sick.

I was learning how to walk in Kingdom authority in my park, but Karen would be getting her training in another place. Remember when we asked God for on-the-job training? Well, Karen was about to get on-the-job training, but it wasn't the job she envisioned.

Karen began to grow weary in waiting for that new car she desperately needed. She didn't just need a car, she needed money. Money to pay down acquired debt and to cover all of their basic needs. "God, I'm praying, I'm declaring, I'm asking, where is my answer?" she continued to question.

Karen needed a job, but she was waiting on her dream. It was like that story of the guy in the flood, stuck on the roof of his house, praying for God to save him. Every time a boat would come by he would say, "No thanks, I'm waiting on God. I'm waiting on my miracle." He couldn't understand that it *was* God who sent him those boats.

Sometimes the delay in our solution is because we don't want to hear the answer God is giving us. Karen didn't want to get a "regular job," she wanted the dream—now! But when she could stand the suffering no more, she finally surrendered. "Okay God, if this is what I am to do, you are going to have to work out all the details."

Early on a Monday morning, she was off to find a job. Her son had to drive her from place to place since she didn't have her own car. Karen has had many years of retail sales experience, so that seemed to be the obvious choice. She first checked out a few places that didn't feel right, but then she stepped into a big department store where a woman in the men's fragrance department said, "Are you coming for a job? We need you here!"—that was weird, and you know what we say about weird.

God *did* work out all the details. I often wondered what it would be like to go back and do things all over again, knowing what I know and who I am now. Karen was about to get that chance. Karen was once again a working woman with a much needed paycheck. She was the newest commissioned employee in the shoe department of a major retailer. It wasn't where she wanted to be, but she trusted God. She would sometimes equate her experience to the biblical story of Joseph—the part where he spent time in the prison. I wonder how Joseph would have felt about that comparison.

Karen may have been different, a new person, but the world was the same. She walked into a department filled with sales people who didn't like the idea of getting some new competition. Karen was in the process of learning how to walk out her new identity, and it was not easy. When she became worried and fearful of not being able to keep up with the others, and make enough sales, Karen had to remember who she was now. When other sales people would deliberately steal sales from her, instead of cursing them, she would ask God to bless them. She may have wanted to slap them a few times, but instead, she prayed for them. When she wanted to give up, instead she spoke peace and blessing over her department. If she was going to live the big life she believed God had for her, she would have to go through the refining process.

All of Karen's prayer began to show fruit. Karen became one of the top producers in her department, and God arranged many unusual and unexpected opportunities for her to pray and speak encouragement into people's lives.

Still, commission sales can be tough, and Karen needed to learn how to rest in God, and on His promises. On a busy Saturday, she noticed that some of her co-workers were feverishly running around grabbing every customer. Karen knew that it wasn't right. It wasn't as it should be. She shouldn't have to run around like a chicken with it's head cut off, just to make a sale. So she stopped and quietly prayed, "God, You show me how to do this the Kingdom way." Right away, she felt at peace. After that, the sales came easy. Instead of Karen chasing customers, they would actually come find her.

But, it wouldn't *always* be that easy. Don't forget, we were in "the process," the place of learning and testing. If we expect God to give us better jobs and bigger assignments, we would first have to show that we could make it through the small beginnings.

One day, Karen called and told me that she had been receiving an unusual number of returns. Returned sales equals less money in her paycheck. Instead of getting frustrated, she said, "God, I know you're always talking to me, and trying to teach me something, what are you telling me?" Instantly, she knew that she was to pray and declare that everything that has been stolen from her be returned. She wasn't just referring to lost sales, she was asking for everything that had been stolen from her life. Not just stolen "things," stolen time, stolen opportunities, and anything else that should have been hers. As soon as she began to declare those words, she heard a customer say, "Order double!" That customer may have been talking about a shoe order, but Karen knew those words—order double, were really meant for her. So, she began to declare that she receive a double portion of all that had been stolen.

The next three customers that Karen helped, each purchased two pairs of shoes—a double portion. If Karen had been all upset about those returns and just complained, like she may have in her past, she probably would have missed out on what God wanted for her. It's an example of why we always need to stay alert and be able to hear the voice of God in every situation. Karen knew that it was about more than her sales. She knew that she needed to keep declaring those words over every area of her life.

Because Karen stayed sensitive to the voice of God, when the biggest return came, instead of getting distracted by her lost commission, she discerned that her customer was distressed. He said that he was returning the shoes because his wife was in the hospital and wouldn't be able to wear shoes like that for a long time. "What happened?" Karen asked. He told her that he and his wife had been in a serious car accident. Karen knew that God had sent him her way, and began to pray over him. Just like Joseph, in the prison, Karen continued to use the tools God had given her.

Finally, after just a few months at the new job, Karen knew it was time to get that car. Yay! Again, God worked out all the details. It may not have been that little red convertible Mercedes she had dreamed of, and still plans to own one day, but it was a brand new little black sports car. She was quite happy. She had been in need of that car for a *very* long time, but it didn't come until she aligned herself with God's plan.

Both of us had been learning how to walk in and steward all the things that God had taught us. How to be Kingdom carriers. How to change the atmosphere and the world around us.

And then, God said, "Now come up higher!"

Chapter 12

The Next 19 Days

It was time to go to the next level. God used Uncle Dave's 19 days of prayer to propel him into his destiny, and to inspire us to find our destiny. It was time for us to go deeper and higher. It was time for the "Next 19 days."

It started with another adventure to Glory of Zion. That's right! We went back to that wild place. We had now been there enough times to no longer be shocked by the many dancing flag wavers or the shofar horn blowers. Believe it or not, we actually felt at home this time. To our own surprise, these radical believing, Word of God speaking, not afraid to dance before the Lord people had become our people. We knew that we were supposed to be in that service that Sunday morning, but didn't know exactly why until Dutch Sheets began to speak. It was a powerful service filled with prophecy, decrees, and proclamations. Heaven opened up and released something major into the atmosphere that day. It was one of those times where you know that there were many mighty angels on assignment and something really big happened, but only God knows all the details. In the midst of it all was a call, a call to worship. Dutch spoke on how 90 days of worship had completely changed him. How worship had not only brought him back to the place of first love, but into a deeper more powerful place, deeper and yet higher. And how in that higher place his perspective was much greater and new revelation came. As he continued to tell us about what those days of worship had done for him, we couldn't wait to get out of that service and run to that place.

Just like Karen had felt when she read about Uncle Dave's 19 days of prayer, and just like I felt when I heard about Karen's days of prayer, we were again feeling that same excited desperation and expectation. But this time was very different; we now had a foundation built under us. We know who we are in Jesus. We have a new identity. Even though we still live in a fallen world, we have the tools to war. This time we were equipped for so much more and we were ready for the next level.

It was time for the *next* 19 days. The first 19 days of prayer was all about building a relationship with God and gaining our true identity. Because of those first days, we now live in a committed relationship with the One who created Heaven and earth, and that in itself is quite awesome, but with God, there's always more.

This time, "The Next 19 Days," was all about worship. God called us into committing to 19 days of worship. It wasn't about giving up prayer, prayer is essential, prayer is calling forth God's will. But now, God wanted to teach us about the power of worship. When we pray, we're usually focused on our wants and needs. When we worship, we focus *only* on Him. Whether it be in word, song, or in other various ways, worship is all about expressing our love and awe for God.

For the next 19 days Karen and I committed to wake up very early each morning to spend time in worship. God knew that for Karen and me, waking up very early each morning would be a big deal, a serious sacrificial commitment. We are girls who can easily stay up very late, but waking up early, well let's just say that only being desperate for more and the fear of God made it possible.

I would set my alarm for 5:00 a.m. each morning, find a quiet spot in my house where I wouldn't wake my family, and quietly play my favorite worship music downloads on my iPhone as I began to worship. Karen also plugged into her favorite worship music each morning and quietly went to the couch in her living room. On one unusual morning, I awoke at exactly 3:33 a.m. For Karen and me, 333 always brings Jeremiah 33:3 to mind. *"Call unto me, and I will answer you, and show you great and mighty things, which you know not."* To me, it was no coincidence that I woke at that exact time. I jumped out of bed and ran to my quiet spot. I didn't even need to play my music that morning because the worship began to freely flow out of me. It felt different than any other time of worship. I can't put it into words, but it was powerful, and I hoped it would happen again.

During those 19 days, we didn't see angels or anything supernatural, but things were indeed happening. For me, it started one day with Jerry, the crossing guard. A few other moms and I would often meet at the school to walk before our kids were dismissed. We would always pass Jerry, the crossing guard, on the busiest street near the school. We usually said hi and maybe mentioned the weather or made a silly comment about walking, but nothing more. On this particular day, Jerry pointed directly at *me* as four of us walked toward him. "Do you work at the school? The cars are going too fast. They're not slowing down." He anxiously said looking at me as if he imagined *I* had the authority to do something about it. I told him that I didn't work at the school, but I would definitely tell someone about the situation.

Later that afternoon, I again ran into Jerry in the parking lot at the grocery store. When I said, "Hi, Jerry!" he grabbed my hand and again said, "The cars are going too fast in the school zone. Something has to be done before someone gets hurt." "Okay, I've got direct access to the boss." I told him. When I said, "boss" I meant God, but he didn't know that.

"Okay God, that was weird, I hear you," I said to myself as I walked away. I knew I had just been given an assignment. On my way home I drove up and down that busy street praying that the cars would slow down and that every child and adult crossing that street would have protection.

The next day, Jerry said that there was a police presence in the school zone that morning, but as soon as they left the cars began to drive fast again. I was thankful for the police presence, but still a bit disappointed. So again, I silently prayed. That afternoon, as I was once again driving and praying on that section of road, God showed me the problem. It was a very dull flashing school zone light. I immediately called the city to report on the dull light. Very early the next morning, the light was replaced! Jerry had a big smile on his face, and actually gave me a bow as the other moms and I walked toward him that afternoon.

God used this small but very serious incident to teach me. I wondered if there would have been a terrible accident in that intersection had I not obeyed what I knew was the voice of God telling me to act. Prayer is always the first action to take, but then I had to see it through. In this case, it meant taking physical action as well. I knew God had appointed me to do something. I knew the protocol. Pray first, and then listen for direction. Because I continued to pray, I was on high alert and could see what God was showing me to do. God gave me a strategic plan and I knew I had the authority to complete it.

Just a day later, In the middle of our 19 days of worship, my son and a friend came running into the house yelling, "Corbin is hurt, he needs you!" Corbin is one of the many kids that play in the park behind our home. He was on my prayer list of 51 kids that I had been praying for. As I ran outside, I saw that he was lying on the ground crying, while his friends worriedly sat next to him. He had just flipped over his bicycle and was in a lot of pain. Without hesitation I said, "Corbin, I'm going to pray for you" and I began to pray. I surprised myself, because before that moment, I hadn't prayed for someone out-loud in public. It was another breakthrough moment.

My house was not the closest house with an

available mom. I asked my son why they came for *me*? He said, "I don't know. I just heard all the other kids yelling; Leif, go get *your* mom!"

These encounters reminded me of how Karen and I use to say, "God, if we are the Whosoevers that you say we are, then why don't the people around us see it or sense it?" Now, it *was* happening.

As our 19 days continued, things were changing in Karen's house as well. She was experiencing breakthrough in her family and with their finances. It started one morning when she gathered her husband and children before work and school, anointed them with oil, and prayed and decreed that breakthrough would come. Her son needed a job, and her husband needed more business. Within just a few days both prayers were answered.

Those 19 days of worship brought us into a higher level of identity. We were gaining new ground. God expanded my small park territory to my neighborhood when on Day 19 my Home Owners Association recruited me to become a board member. I had already been prayer-walking my neighborhood, but this was different. To me it wasn't just another thing I had on my agenda. It was an invitation to expand my territory of authority in prayer.

At my first HOA meeting, I met someone who would become my neighborhood prayer partner.

Along with my usual daily prayer-walks, she and I would meet up every Tuesday evening to prayer-walk the neighborhood together. By now, I knew how to do it. What I didn't know back then was that my new prayer-partner was a bit shocked by the way I prayed. Having been raised a Baptist preacher's kid, she said that she was used to hearing sad or pathetic woe-is-me types of prayers. She told me that she was amazed by my boldness. She confided, "Laurie, you were prophesying and praying prayers of declarations like I had never heard before."

I didn't know, until a year later when we had this conversation, that it had been such an unusual experience for her. "Did you think I was crazy?" I asked. She laughed and said, "Well, only for a little while, but then I began to see the tangible results." She reminded me about the day I had told her that we were going to change the atmosphere in our neighborhood, and that we absolutely did do that. She also reminded me of how we not only could feel the change, but could even see a literal change in people's yards.

During those prayer walks I always prayed "Kingdom come, and God's will be done in this neighborhood," but there were very specific prayers as well. My new prayer partner had lived in the neighborhood for many years and knew a lot of the neighborhood family issues: Divorce, drugs, sickness, financial issues, etc... So we would pray for forgiveness, healing, restoration, freedom from addictions and poverty, blessing and protection, and much more. Together we completed some serious intercession for our neighborhood, but most importantly for our neighbors. And just like with the park, neighbors would stop to talk and unknowingly put in their prayer requests.

My prayer partner friend recently said, "Laurie, I would go home and pray over my own home and family the same way you would pray over the neighborhood." She told me that it completely flipped her world around. Her husband and kids immediately began to see the change in her and they began to change as well. Apparently, that new identity I was walking in was highly contagious.

While I was taking more territory in my neighborhood, Karen was on another mission. All along this journey, Karen kept hearing God calling her to pray for the family, the bloodline, to be more specific. Every time she would think she was finished, God would bring her right back to it again. Now, finally, after years of not being able to shake this thing that felt like a burden, instead of running from the family legacy, God was showing her how to embrace it. God was teaching Karen that if she would pray for all those that Uncle Dave and our Grandmother had covered in prayer, she would find her own healing as well. She prayed for everyone by name. She prayed for protection and blessing, but mostly, she asked God to give them revelation of who He was. When she didn't know what to pray, God would somehow always give her the words and the strategy to pray. Just like my neighborhood prayer, Karen was praying for forgiveness, healing, restoration, and wholeness. Nehemiah 4:14 tells us to *remember the Lord who is great and glorious, and fight for your families.* She was praying for generational forgiveness and healing. She was praying for a release of things that have been locked up. She was praying for bloodline promises that were never attained.

We've mentioned our Uncle Dave, but our family legacy actually began generations before him. Our mom, Ruth Wilkerson Harris, wrote *The Wilkerson Legacy,* a book that tells the story of those earlier generations. We're proud to say that it wasn't just the men, but there were many bold prayer-warrior women in our bloodline as well.

Soon after our 19 days of worship, Susan, our younger sister, called to tell us that our dad had suffered a mild stroke. She said that Dad was having trouble putting words together, and when he sat down at the piano, the place of his worship, he wasn't able to play. Sickness, of any sort, is never from God. Both Karen and I knew it was not just a physical thing, but a spiritual attack as well. We became filled with a righteous anger as we immediately began to war over our dad. Just a couple of weeks earlier, I had two dreams about Dad and his piano. In one dream something was blocking the sound from coming forth. In the other, as he played a worship song on the piano, I told him that worship equaled encountering God. I didn't really know what these dreams meant at the time, but now it was obvious.

There's a great Bible verse in Matthew that says, *"The kingdom of Heaven suffers violence, and the violent take it by force."* Satan trying to steal Dad's worship was the thing that really magnified the "NO!" the take-it-by-force in us. It heightened our warring. We knew that through those 19 days of worship, God had prepared and equipped us for this moment. Karen and I had a confident faith that we would win this fight. The three of us went into battle mode. We each spent time praying, decreeing, and truth be told—sometimes crying. Karen told Susan that we'll know we've reached a breakthrough when she calls and says, Dad's playing the piano again. And just a couple of days later, Karen answered her phone to hear the sound of Susan quietly crying. Dad was powerfully playing one of his favorite worship hymns on the piano. Karen says that she will never forget that moment. God is *always* good!

Not too many years ago, we felt weak and powerless, but not anymore. God has loved us, equipped us, and empowered us to be, not only Kingdom carriers, but Kingdom enforcers.

Worship is the key! Now, our prayer time, one-to-One, always begins with a time of worship. Worship comes first because that's what brings us into God's presence and when we can hear Him best. It's the place where God gives us a download of wisdom and revelation. Then, instead of praying just what we want to pray, we're able to pray the things that God wants us to pray. We pray and say the things that he reveals to us in worship.

Now we know, it was never about the material stuff or riding on anyone's coattails. It was always about finding our rightful Kingdom identities, and standing on the shoulders of those who came before us. We can now say, **"I am Whosoever!"** with great authority and boldness.

So for you, Uncle Dave, we say, "We honor you. We stand on your shoulders so that we can reach even higher. And we pray, that we too can be the shoulders that our children, our grandchildren, our nieces and nephews, and others will stand on and reach for more."

God has so much more for us, and though we don't yet know all that He has in store, we do know that it will be born of God, it will be built on worship, and it will be dependent on prayer.

We pray

that God may grant you a spirit
of wisdom and revelation [of insight into mysteries
and secrets] in the [deep and intimate] knowledge of
Him, by having the eyes of your heart flooded with
light, so that you can know *and* understand the hope
to which He called you, and how rich is His glorious
inheritance in the saints (His set-apart ones), and [so
that you can know and understand] what is the im-
measurable *and* unlimited *and* surpassing greatness
of His power in *and* for us who believe.

Ephesians 1:17-19

Made in the USA
San Bernardino, CA
05 May 2015